THE
LITTLE
BOOK
OF
MAYO

EAMONN HENRY

To the Mayo Senior Football Team and its Quest for Sam:
Keep the Faith!

First published 2016

The History Press Ireland
50 City Quay
Dublin 2
Ireland
www.thehistorypress.ie

The History Press Ireland are a member of Publishing Ireland,
the Irish Book Publisher's Association.

© Eamonn Henry, 2016

The right of Eamonn Henry to be identified as the Author
of this work has been asserted in accordance with the
Copyright, Designs and Patents Act 1988.

British Library Cataloguing in Publication Data.
A catalogue record for this book is available from the British Library.

ISBN 978 1 84588 892 3

Typesetting and origination by The History Press
Printed and bound by TJ International Ltd.

CONTENTS

FOREWORD

I took my seat on the plane at Knock airport on a cold, wet and windy day in the late 1980s. My fellow passengers slowly made their way to their seats and settled in. As I fastened my seatbelt I noticed that the young woman seated beside me was in some distress. Tears rolled down her cheeks as she tried to peer out through the steamed-up window of the aeroplane. When I enquired as to the cause of her misery she made the tearful reply, 'It's my first time leaving home', as she wiped the condensation from the windowpane.

I glanced through the window to get a clearer picture of this place that the young woman called home. The wind blew, and the rain, horizontal at times, whistled round the hillocks of Barrnacúige. Even the sheep turned their backsides towards the wind, as did a lone mountain ash that still clung to the outer edge of the airport runway. And beyond that, a broad expanse of wet, brown bog led my gaze towards Charlestown and farther afield, while the distant houses appeared as white specks on this rain-drenched landscape.

What was it about this place, I wondered, that would cause this young woman to shed such tears. Certainly not the calm days and scorching sunshine, I mused. What could it be? Was it the breaking of ties, with family and friends and familiar places, or the memories of youth and happy times, which might now be lost, or was it something more than that? Could it be the histories of previous generations who had hewn a living from the sides of the mountain, smallholdings marked with their sweat, and called it home? Or, was it all of these?

Whatever it was, it was a potent mix, I reckoned. Perhaps it could be bottled and labelled 'Essence of Mayo'.

These heartfelt ties that Mayo people have to their native county are complex and raw and do not always lend themselves to easy analysis. In the *Little Book of Mayo*, however, Eamonn Henry endeavours to tease out the historical and emotional ties that bind us to this small piece of earth that we call home. His chapter on the quest for the Sam Maguire Cup best exemplifies this pride in place that Mayo people display to an almost obsessive degree. If you want to see thousands of grown men cry, then come to Croke Park on the third Sunday in September where Mayo are six points ahead with only minutes of the All-Ireland Football Final left to play. It is also the case, sadly, that the tears are even more heartfelt at the final whistle! Undoubtedly, the 'Quest for Sam' is among the strongest ties that bind Mayo people throughout the world to their home place.

Reading through this book, it is quite apparent that Mayo is the place to visit. St Patrick spent some time here in the fifth century, from his youthful escapade in Killala to his later sojourn in Ballintubber on his way to the Reek. Centuries later we even had a visit from Mary, the mother of God, who appeared to a small group in the little village of Knock in 1879. But that wasn't enough! In order to balance things up, the Devil himself put in an appearance at the dance hall in Tooreen, in the late 1950s. In the chapter 'The Night the Devil Appeared in Tooreen', Eamonn Henry paints an intriguing picture of the social mores of the time and the influence of the Catholic Church on the everyday lives of the people.

The story of Mayo is a story of emigration, and that emigrant story features in many chapters of this book. From the earliest times through the famine years, throughout the twentieth century, hundreds of thousands have left this place, many driven out by poverty or landlords, leaving their smouldering hovels behind them. In later years they had their American wakes, bid their families farewell, often for the last time, and made new lives in the land of dreams. Today 34 million Americans claim Irish ancestry, among whom are many with roots in County Mayo.

In post-war Britain many seasonal workers from Mayo found employment, whether 'tatie-hoking' in Scotland, haymaking in Yorkshire or beet-pulling in Lincolnshire. Many others moved to Britain more permanently to work in the construction industry or the National Health Service. Their remittances, 'wired home' at the end of the week, helped to sustain their families through tough economic times. The children and grandchildren of those men and women from Mayo, who landed at Holyhead in the 1950s and '60s, are now found in positions of power and influence in British society, such as in politics, in business or playing soccer in the Premier League.

There is so much more in this *Little Book of Mayo* that the reader will wish to explore. The author provides a comprehensive description of landscape, geology and those natural features best known to the seasoned traveller as well as those lesser-known havens off the tourist trail. He presents interesting background information on Mayo men and women, many of whom have played prominent and public roles, including Granuaile, who, barefooted, held a meeting with Queen Elizabeth I in London, our current Taoiseach Enda Kenny from Castlebar, and former President Mary Robinson from Ballina, who continues to influence international affairs.

By the end of the book, Eamonn Henry leads us to the present time to provide a view of life in County Mayo today. Industry and commerce are developing steadily while tourism increases exponentially. Today's visitors are drawn to Westport House, the number one attraction in the county and, ironically, a striking legacy of colonial times. The other main attractions include Croagh Patrick, Knock Shrine and the Céide Fields. A more recent tourist destination to gain international recognition is the Wild Atlantic Way. It was always there, of course, stretching from Cork to Donegal, but the new brand provides a signpost for the traveller who wishes to experience the raw and rugged coastline of Mayo.

This book has something for everybody, especially for those with an interest in the county or who may wish to visit. I commend it wholeheartedly to the reader.

Tom McAndrew

ACKNOWLEDGEMENTS

In researching this book I received help from a number of people whose assistance I wish to acknowledge.

First and foremost, I would like to thank Ivor Hamrock, Local Studies Librarian at Mayo County Library in Castlebar. Ivor has been most helpful, giving me research tips and providing access to documents within the library and elsewhere. Without his assistance and advice, my work would have been much more difficult.

Rosa Meehan's epic work *The Tale of Mayo* was a great addition to the list of resources that I used. Anyone looking for a comprehensive guide to all things Mayo will not find a better one than this fine work.

The chapter, 'Ballintubber Abbey', is largely based on *The Story of Ballintubber Abbey* by Revd Thomas Regan. I also had a most informative conversation with Muriel, one of the abbey staff, when I visited the place recently.

Through Fagan's Gates by Tom Higgins was a great source of Castlebar-related information as was Ivor Hamrock's, *Castlebar Gaol*.

I found much useful information on a number of websites. The sites of Mayo County Council and the Mayo County Library deserve special mention. The same can be said for mayo-ireland.com, a very comprehensive Mayo-based site.

When researching the subject of Granuaile, the Pirate Sea-Queen, I found much useful information at ireland-calling.com and www.ocean-of-storms.com.

My late father, John Henry, was a noted folk historian and archivist and I have quoted extensively from his work throughout this book. (Further details can be had from mayofolktales.com.)

Another fine site for historical information can be found at www.libraryireland.com.

I have referred to *A Topographical Dictionary of Ireland*, by Samuel Lewis, several times throughout this book, as well as quoting extensively from it in the penultimate chapter 'Samuel Lewis: The Topography of Mayo'.

I used material from 'Parks and Gardens in Ireland' and also from the Ballycroy National Park website when writing about this national park (*www.ireland101.com/page/parksandgardens* & *www.ballycroynationalpark.ie/*).

I used extracts from the History Ireland site when writing about the Revd Edward Nangle.

Finally, I would like to acknowledge the assistance of my good friend and fellow Mayophile, Tom McAndrew. Apart from writing the foreword, Tom acted as proofreader and devil's advocate, as well as providing that vital second perspective that *The Little Book of Mayo*, and works of a similar nature, require. It could be said that, while I drafted this book, Tom crafted it.

1

THE GEOGRAPHY OF COUNTY MAYO

Mayo is a maritime county in the north-west of Ireland, in the province of Connacht. It is bounded to the north and west by the Atlantic Ocean and it borders Sligo, Roscommon and Galway to the south and east.

It is the third largest of Ireland's thirty-two counties in area but only 15th in terms of population. It is the second largest of Connacht's five counties in both size and population. Mayo, including the islands, has the longest coastline of all the Irish maritime counties, at 725 miles (1,168km).

TOWNS OF MAYO

The largest towns of Mayo in order of population size are:

Castlebar	10,835
Ballina	10,354
Westport	5,543
Claremorris	3,979
Ballinrobe	3,682
Ballyhaunis	3,008
Swinford	2,607
Kiltimagh	1,507
Foxford	1,326
Belmullet	1,089

(Figures based on 2011 Census Returns)

GEOLOGY OF MAYO

Rock Types

The Mayo landscape is varied and this is no surprise, given the complicated geological foundation that lies beneath. (The geology of a region largely determines the nature of the soil and the principal features of the landscape, such as the mountains, rivers and lakes.)

Luckily for the country as a whole, the mountains along the western coastline of the county are amongst the oldest and most weather-resistant rocks to be found anywhere in the country. Were this not so, the softer, low-lying limestone plains to the east of this mountain barrier of igneous and metamorphic structures would prove no match for the ceaseless pounding of the Atlantic waves.

To the south of Clew Bay, the geological makeup is very complex with a series of rock folds and extrusions of metamorphic rock, signs of the massive magma movements millions of years ago. Here, a fault runs between Croagh Patrick and the southern shore of Clew Bay. This is the main branch of the Highland Boundary Zone, which, beginning at Clew Bay and extending across the country in a north-eastern direction, extends as far as Scotland.

Annagh Head on the Mullet Peninsula and the Broadhaven Stags are folded gneiss and are virtually erosion-resistant. They are over 1,750 million years old.

To the north of Clew Bay, metamorphic rocks predominate. Schist is the most common form. A broad strip of fertile limestone plains extends from Killala in north Mayo south to Cong on the Mayo-Galway border. The limestone region extends eastwards into the Midland Plains with the Ox Mountains bordering it to the north-east of the county. This mountain range is composed mainly of granite with gneiss and schist outcrops in places.

Climate

Ice has played a large part in the formation of the Mayo landscape and so have the combined forces of wind and water. Glaciers carved out great mountain valleys, known as glaciated troughs, with steep, straight sides and a flat bottom.

In the region north-east of Swinford in east Mayo, the geological rock type is limestone but it has been overgrown with peat. This area of raised bog extends into County Sligo.

The quality of the soils in this part of the county is also adversely affected by the belt of drumlins and eskers deposited there by retreating glaciers during the last Ice Age. Those mounds of sand and gravel deposits, left behind as the ice melted, stretch west to Clew Bay. The myriad of tiny islands in the bay is sunken drumlins, partly submerged as sea levels rose.

Since the Ice Age ended, the landscape has undergone continuous change, caused by the weather systems of the Atlantic and also by water. Rivers have created valleys and lakes and the sea is continually reworking the coast, eroding the coastline in places and building beaches in others.

OTHER PHYSICAL FEATURES

Principal Rivers
The *Moy* is the longest river in the county and from source to sea is roughly 62 miles (100km) long. It rises in the Ox Mountains in Sligo and flows into Killala Bay, north of Ballina. It is undeniably the best salmon-fishing river in the country.

The *Deel* rises in the Nephin Beg Mountains and is 28 miles (45km) long. It flows through the town of Crossmolina, before entering the northern end of Lough Conn. It is the largest of the Moy tributaries and offers a wide variety of angling experiences, ranging from dry fly fishing for trout to spring salmon fishing.

The *Robe* rises in Bekan, near Ballyhaunis, and empties into Lough Mask. It is over 37 miles (60km) long and is a noted brown-trout river.

The *Clare* also rises near Ballyhaunis and flows southwards for 58 miles (93km) before flowing into Lough Corrib in County Galway. It is popular with salmon and trout anglers.

Bays

Killala Bay lies between County Mayo and County Sligo. It is the estuary of the River Moy. The village of Killala is situated on its western shore. It is an excellent fishing location. *Bartragh Island* is situated in the centre of the bay.

Broadhaven Bay is a natural bay of the Atlantic Ocean situated on the north-western coast of Mayo. The bay faces northwards, stretching 5 miles (8.6km) between Erris Head in the west and Kid Island in the east. The landscape largely consists of Atlantic blanket bog interspersed with some areas of sandy grassland habitats and white sandy beaches.

Blacksod Bay in Erris, north Mayo, is 10 miles (16km) long and 5 miles (8km) wide and is bounded on its western side by the Mullet Peninsula. Its eastern side includes Kiltane parish, which extends southwards from Belmullet towards Geesala and Doohoma.

Keem Bay is located past Dooagh village in the west of Achill Island. It contains a Blue Flag beach. The bay was formerly the site of a basking shark fishery. To the west is an old booley village at Bunown. To the north stands Croaghaun, with Europe's highest cliffs. The beach is sheltered and offers opportunities for snorkelling.

Clew Bay is an ocean bay on the west coast of the county. It contains Ireland's best example of sunken drumlins. The bay is overlooked by Croagh Patrick to the south and the Nephin Range Mountains in north Mayo. Clare Island straddles the entrance to the bay. From the southwest part of the bay eastwards are Louisburgh, Lecanvey, Murrisk and Westport; north of Westport is Newport, and westwards from there lies Mulranny, the gateway to Achill.

Killary Harbour is a fjord located in the heart of Connemara. It forms a natural border between counties Galway and Mayo. It is 10 miles (16km) long and at its centre over 147 feet (45m) deep. It is the only natural glacial fjord in Ireland.

Headlands of County Mayo
Benwee Head, with its cliffs, arches, stacks and islands, offers some of the most dramatic coastal scenery in Ireland. These cliffs tower over Broadhaven Bay. To appreciate the cliffs fully, one needs to see them from the sea. Benwee Head is in the townland of Kilgalligan in the parish of Kilcommon. An Bhinn Bhuí is the most northerly summit in the north Mayo area.

Erris Head is a promontory at the northernmost tip of the Mullet Peninsula. It is a well-known and recognised landmark used by mariners and weather forecasters. It is also a very scenic viewpoint, with an unspoilt view of the Atlantic Ocean and steep rocky cliffs.

Downpatrick Head is located between the town of Ballycastle and the Céide Fields, further west. It lies in an area of outstanding natural beauty, including the spectacular sea stack of Dún Briste.

Islands of County Mayo
Achill Island is the largest island off the coast of Ireland and is situated off the Mayo coast. It has a population of 2,700. Its area is 57 miles^2

(148km²). The island is 87 per cent peat bog. Achill is attached to the mainland by the Michael Davitt Bridge, between the villages of Achill Sound and Polranny. A bridge was first built here in 1887, replaced by another structure in 1949 and subsequently replaced with the current bridge, which was completed in 2008.

Other centres of population include the villages of Keel, Dooagh, Dooega, and Dugort. The parish's main Gaelic football pitch and two secondary schools are on the mainland at Polranny.

Early human settlements are believed to have been established on Achill around 3000 BC. A paddle dating from this period was found at the crannóg near Dookinella. The parish of Achill also includes the Corraun Peninsula. There are between 500 and 600 native Irish speakers in Achill parish.

Achill Beg is a small island just off the southern tip of Achill Island. It was evacuated in 1965 and the inhabitants were settled on the main (Achill) island and nearby mainland.

Clare Island is a mountainous island guarding the entrance to Clew Bay in County Mayo. It is famous as the home of the pirate queen, Granuaile. Approximately 145 people live there today.

The Inishkea Islands are situated off the coast of the Mullet Peninsula. There are two main islands – Inishkea North and Inishkea South. The islands lie between Inishglora to their north and Duvillaun to their

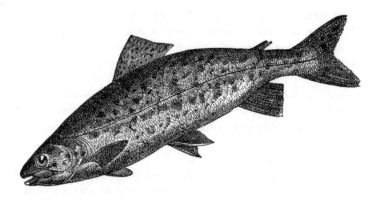

south, off the Mullet's west coast, and offer some protection to the mainland coast from the power of the Atlantic Ocean. The underlying rocks of the Inishkea Islands are gneiss and schist, the same as that on the Mullet. The islands are relatively low-lying. Fine white sand is to be found everywhere, often blown into drifts by the strong winds, especially along the beach beside the harbour, where it fills the houses of the abandoned village. The inhabitants of both Inishkea North and South left the islands in the 1930s after most of their young men died at sea in a storm.

The islands lie about 9 miles (15km) off the mainland; their highest point reaches 189.3m above sea level. Between Inishturk and Clare Island lies Caher Island. It has a population of fifty-eight people. There are two main settlements, both on the more sheltered eastern end of the island, Ballyheer and Garranty.

Lakes of County Mayo

Lough Conn, along with *Lough Cullin*, covers about 14,000 acres (5,665 hectares). It is connected to Lough Cullin, to the south by a narrow waterway. Lough Cullin, in turn, drains into the River Moy and thence to the Atlantic. Lough Conn is noted for its trout and salmon fishing. World Fly Fishing Tournaments have been held on this lake on several occasions.

Lough Mask is a lake of approximately 20,500 acres (8,296 hectares) in south Mayo, due north of Lough Corrib. It is the middle one of three lakes, all of which empty into the Corrib River, flowing through Galway and into Galway Bay. Lough Mask is the sixth largest lake, by area, in Ireland. The eastern half of Lough Mask is shallow and contains many islands. The other half is much deeper, sinking to a long trench with depths in excess of 164ft (50m). It is the largest lake, by water volume, in the Republic of Ireland.

Lough Carra flows into Lough Mask, which in turn feeds into Lough Corrib through an underground stream that emerges in Cong village and becomes the River Cong.

Mountains and Hills of Mayo

Croagh Patrick, nicknamed 'The Reek', is a 2,500ft (764m) high mountain and an important site of pilgrimage in County Mayo. It is 5 miles (8km) from Westport and towers above the villages of Murrisk and Lecanvey. Every year, it is climbed by pilgrims on Reek Sunday, which is the last Sunday in July. It forms the southern part of a U-shaped valley created by a glacier flowing into Clew Bay in the last Ice Age.

Croaghaun is a mountain on Achill Island. At +2,257ft (+688m), it has the highest sea cliffs in Ireland and Great Britain. Its cliffs are on the northern slope of the mountain. The cliffs can only be seen by climbing to the summit of the mountain or from the sea. They are part of a sequence of sheer rock faces which start south of Keem Bay and loop around the uninhabited north-west of the island, by Achill Head and Saddle Head, and east to Slievemore, occasionally dropping vertically into the waters of the Atlantic.

Knockmore is a mountain on Clare Island, off the coast of Mayo. The mountain is the highest peak on Clare Island at 1,516ft (462m). It is a popular walking destination and is famous for its view of Clew Bay and the west coast.

Maamtrasma is a mountain among the Partry Hills. With an elevation of 2,237ft (682m), it is famous for its breath-taking scenery.

Mweelrea is the highest mountain in Connacht and lies to the north of Killary Harbour.

Nephin, at 2,646ft (806m), is the second-highest peak in Connacht. It is to the west of Lough Conn.

Nephin Beg is a mountain in the Nephin Beg Range, which lies west of Lough Conn and north-west of Newport. While it takes its name from Nephin, that mountain is some distance away and there are intervening mountains between them. Its highest point is 2,057ft (627m).

Peninsulas of County Mayo
The Corraun Peninsula is on the west coast of the county. It is located between the mainland and the island of Achill. There are great views from there of Clew Bay and the *Mullet Peninsula* to the north.

HUMAN IMPACT ON THE LANDSCAPE

In relatively recent times, man has made dramatic changes to the landscape. By clearing trees, early farmers facilitated the growth of peat land. The bogs created in this fashion were altered in turn by the removal of turf for fuel and, in places, by the planting of coniferous trees.

Canals have been dug and bridges and roads have been built across bog and mountain, as well as through fertile plains, bringing change in their wake as people used the changes to their own advantage.

TRANSPORT

Rail
The Midland and Great Western Railway laid the first railway line in Mayo in 1861. It connected Castlerea in County Roscommon to Ballyhaunis in south Mayo.

Some 2,000 people were employed to bring the railway to Ballyhaunis. In May 1862, the line reached Claremorris and in December 1862 it was extended to Castlebar. Four years later, this line was extended to Westport, with an extension to Westport Quay opened in 1874.

The northern extension from Manulla was begun with the opening of the line to Foxford in 1868. Ballina was reached in 1873 and an extension to Killala was opened in 1893.

The railway was extended from Westport to Achill Sound in the 1890s. This latter was a narrow-gauge line and was one of the so-called 'Balfour Lines', named after Arthur J. Balfour, Chief Secretary for Ireland during the years 1887–91 and designed to provide employment in disadvantaged areas. The line to Achill was completed in May 1895.

The first station on this extension was Newport, which opened in February 1894 upon the completion of a nearby tunnel at the end of Newport station. It was closed in September 1937. While most of the line has been converted to Greenway, the tunnel remains closed.

There is a rather tragic twist to the story of the Westport-Achill railway line. Local legend has it that a seventeenth-century poet and mystic, Brian Rua Ó Cearbháin, predicted that, *'D'tiocfad an lá nuair a bead rota iarainn ar coirti teinaead o dear agus o tuadh'* ('The day will come when there will be iron wheels on fire carriages from the south and the north').

He also predicted that the first and last train between Westport and Achill would carry dead bodies. The first train that came had the bodies of people who were drowned while transferring from a hooker to board a steamer in Westport.

The last train to run on this line, in 1937, brought the bodies of ten young people who had been burnt to death in Kirkintollach in Scotland. The victims were 'tatie hookers', potato pickers, who had been sleeping in a 'bothy', a ramshackle shed, when the place went on fire. The door of the bothy had been locked and the young victims were trapped inside the burning building.

A New Prosperity

Individual towns prospered with the arrival of the railways in Mayo. When Irish railway companies became involved in the hotel business, the luxury Mulranny Hotel opened in 1897. Thousands of employees worked on the construction of the Mayo rail network and it brought prosperity to towns connected to the system.

The railways facilitated the development of trade and commerce, transporting cattle and dry farm produce to centres outside the county and bringing in materials from other places.

Air

Ireland West Airport Knock is an international airport located in the county. The name is derived from the nearby village of Knock. Recent years have seen the airport's passenger numbers grow to over 750,000 yearly and it has a number of UK and European destinations. August 2014 was its busiest month on record, with 102,774 passengers using the airport.

Belmullet Airstrip

In November 1978, the first small plane landed on the 700-yard (640m) airstrip at Belmullet. Udarás na Gaeltachta, which had been supportive of the project from the start, took over this community-sponsored airstrip in the early 1980s. The local community had worked with Udarás to purchase 12 acres (5 hectares) of land for the airport, which was initially intended as a means of attracting industrial investors to the area. In recent years, it has contributed to the development of a growing tourist trade.

Castlebar Airport

Castlebar has a long history of aviation. William Munnelly of Castlebar and James Mee of Mullingar, who later settled in Castlebar, were among the members of the Royal Flying Corps, forerunners of the Royal Air Corps, who landed regularly in Castlebar during the First World War. After the war, pleasure flights came into vogue and this eventually resulted in the development of Castlebar Regional Airport. In August 1966, a private airport at Castlebar, with a landing strip of over half a mile (1km) long, was opened, with the financial backing of two Mayo brothers, Peter and Hugh Ryan.

Roads

There are a number of national primary roads in the county, including the N5 road connecting Westport with Dublin and the N17 road that connects Galway and Sligo and passes by Knock International Airport.

The N26 road connects Ballina with Dublin via the N5 while the N26 road is a national primary road connecting the N5 road at Swinford with the N58 at Foxford and then on to the N59 road at Ballina. This route is Mayo's second busiest road, after the N5, with almost 10,000 vehicles daily using the route between Ballina and Foxford.

Bridges

Michael Davitt Bridge connects Achill Island to the peninsula. The original structure was a swing bridge pivoting on a central pier and was officially opened by Michael Davitt, the founder of the Land League in 1897. In 1947, it was replaced by another, larger one, also named after Michael Davitt.

The Seven Arches Bridge is a historic railway bridge in Newport. Built around 1892, the bridge is a seven-span, squared, red sandstone structure straddling the Black Oak River. It carried the Westport-to-Achill line before closing in 1937. The bridge is listed as a protected structure.

Pontoon Bridge is located in the picturesque little village of Pontoon, situated between Lough Conn and Lough Cullin, close to the town of Foxford. A narrow water channel carrying the waters of Lough Conn into Lough Cullin runs through the centre of this hamlet. A pontoon bridge of linked, flat-bottomed boats carried traffic across this water channel until a permanent structure was put in place. This new structure retained the name of its predecessor.

Burrishoole Bridge, a seven-arched structure, crosses the Burrishoole Channel. It was built in the eighteenth century as part of the roadway between Newport and Mulranny.

The Salmon Weir Bridge is a pedestrian bridge over the River Moy from Barrett Street to Ridge Pool Road in Ballina. The bridge, which was designed to resemble a fishing rod, was opened in July 2009.

The Clapper Bridge, west of Louisburgh at Bunlahinch, is thought to date from medieval times and is one of the oldest bridges in the county. These bridges were built with long, thin slabs of stone to make a beam-type deck and with large rocks or block-like piles of stones for piers.

The Musical Bridge, Bellacorick, was designed by cartographer and civil engineer William Bald in 1820. It is known as the Musical Bridge as the parapet slabs will emit musical notes if someone strikes any of them with a handheld stone. Each slab has a unique musical note.

Apparently, the bridge was difficult to construct because the ground is very hard and the workmen had great difficulty excavating holes to hold the foundations in place. The bridge has four elliptical arches, each 30ft (9m) apart, with battlements nearly 400ft (120m) long.

The Erris prophet Brian Rua Ó Cearbháin referred to the then unbuilt bridge at Bellacorick in the seventeenth century. He said that it would never be finished and it never has been. A block is missing from one of the parapet walls. According to local tradition, anyone who attempts to lay the last block will die shortly afterwards. It is said locally that a man who did attempt to finish the bridge dropped dead on the spot.

2

CRIME AND PUNISHMENT

Mayo towns were not always considered pleasant places in the middle of the eighteenth century.

Mary McCarthy in her book, *Fighting Fitzgerald*, had this to say about the town of Castlebar at that time:

> The grim little town of Castlebar, the capital of Mayo, had a barracks, a courthouse with a piazza, a jail and at that time a drop or a gibbet on the Mall.
>
> The sound and the clash of steel, or the crack of pistols, could be heard, constantly coming from the barrack yard. County gentlemen fought their duels there.
>
> Castlebar was filled with a cockfighting, dogfighting, gaming, gossiping population; it usually wore an outward air of stagnation, but on a market day, or when petty sessions were on, and on a hanging day, the little town was crowded and the chapel filled. At night the inhabitants were afraid to go by the mall when a corpse was swinging from the gibbet; but in the daytime it was quite usual for people to pass beneath a dead felon.
>
> There was hardly a month without some poor fellow being strapped up for rebellion, theft or some other misdemeanour that would not be lightly punished.

George Robert Fitzgerald, 'Fighting Fitz,' was hanged from this gibbet for the murder of a fellow-landlord, Randall McDonnell. At the height of his pride and popularity in 1783, he was considered the best-dressed dandy in Ireland. Yet, when he went to his execution in 1794, he was described as being dressed in a tattered peasant coat tied with rope and an old caubeen hat tied with a string.

The High Sheriff, Denis Browne (Donnacha an Rópa – Denis of the Rope), who was in charge of the trial, had long been an enemy of the Fitzgeralds. Fitzgerald and his accomplices, Brecknock, and Fulton, were sentenced to be hanged. Two hours after their conviction, Brecknock and Fulton were transported from the gaol, then at the junction of Castle Street and Ellison Street, by cart to the new gaol, the Bridewell, then under construction at The Mall, where they were hanged.

An hour afterwards, Fitzgerald walked to the gallows surrounded by a strong contingent of Browne's men, having been granted this concession to avoid being jeered by the mob of onlookers. His hanging was as dramatic as his life had been.

When all was ready for Fitzgerald's execution, after spending some time in prayer, he leaped impetuously from the scaffold, breaking the rope and breaking a leg.

He shouted, 'My life is my own', according to local tradition. 'Not while there is a rope in Castlebar,' was the grim retort of Denis Browne.

On the second attempt the rope was too long. He was eventually hanged on the third attempt.

Local tradition asserted that a few minutes before Fitzgerald's execution a horseman was seen approaching Castlebar on the Dublin road, trying to urge on his tired horse and waving a piece of paper in his hand.

Denis Browne, according to the story, speeded up the execution. The paper in question was believed to be a pardon for Fitzgerald from the Lord Lieutenant but nothing further was heard of the matter.

ARMY LIFE

Discipline was harsh in the army barracks also. According to the *Castlebar Telegraph*:

One December morning in 1845 the 'loud and agonizing cries of a person apparently in the extremes of bodily torture and anguish' echoed through the streets of Castlebar, County Mayo. In the town's barrack a sergeant of the 30th Regiment was being flogged 100 times by the cat o' nine tails, for the grievous offence of drunkenness on duty. The shrieks and subduing prayers for mercy of the poor fellow were heard distinctly on the bridge and in the town generally.

MAYO GAOLS

There were gaols in different towns in the county, including Cong, Belmullet, Swinford, Ballinrobe and Ballintubber.

The latter two are mentioned in a popular children's rhyme of the period:

> Shake hands, brother
> You're a rogue and I'm another
> You'll be hanged in Ballinrobe
> I'll be hanged in Ballintubber
> You'll be hanged with a rope
> I'll be hanged with a rubber
> The rubber will break
> And I'll be safe
> But you'll be hanged for ever.

The prison standards varied from place to place. The smallness of gaols naturally led to serious overcrowding. In 1777, for instance, in the prison at Castlebar, forty-two prisoners were confined in one room, 21ft (6m) by 17ft (5m). Another reason for overcrowding was the keeping of debtors in gaols that were meant to house only criminals or those so accused. To add to the problem was the fact that it was not uncommon for the families and even servants of debtors to live with them.

During the terrible famine years, the imbalance between the haves and the have-nots was painfully clear; there was one code of law for the rich and a much different one for the poor.

As far as the law was concerned, the right to property took precedence over the right to life, particularly in cases where a landlord's property was held in higher regard than the lives of starving tenants and their families.

The incidence of crime rose during the Great Famine. Most crimes involved the theft of food and were carried out in desperation. There were also attacks on rent and rate collectors. Fifteen thousand extra troops were drafted in to police the country and new laws were enacted.

The County Gaol

According to law, each county in eighteenth-century Ireland had its own prison located in the chief town. In addition some large towns had their own gaols, although at times (to save on expenses) these were used jointly by both town and county. The law also required that every county have a house of correction (usually called a bridewell) where drunkards, petty thieves, rioters and vagrants were held for a few days before trial.

The original Castlebar Gaol was built on the corner of Ellison Street and Castle Lane. In 1835, it was moved to a site on the Westport road.

An English visitor, William Makepeace Thackeray, described the new gaol as being 'like a stately Gothic castle but for the legend above the gate, which read "Without Beware, Within Amend".'

HARD TIMES, DESPERATE TIMES

Even though the economic and moral climate were very different then, the following extract from the *Achill Missionary Herald* in January 1847 is difficult to comprehend:

> We regret extremely to state that a hooker belonging to General Thompson, of Connemara, which put into Achill Sound, at the south of the island, from stress of weather, was plundered by a party of the natives of this island. One person suspected of being concerned in this outrage has been apprehended, and there is reason to hope that others also will be brought to justice. We tell the natives of Achill, and they know that the advice is given by a real friend, that any man among them who engages in such lawless proceedings is the enemy of the whole population. The general good conduct of our poor islanders under their distressing trial is deserving of the highest commendation; the lawless conduct of some to which we have alluded is the only exception.

The driving force behind the paper was Revd Edward Nangle, an evangelical Protestant minister who founded a proselytising mission near Dugort on Achill Island. According to his biographer, Revd Henry Seddal, the two great driving forces in his life were Christ and the Bible. It's hard to see a connection with either Christ or the Bible and the statement that any man who robs food in the middle of a famine is an enemy of the people.

Some people in their desperate search for food resorted to violence, including looting and murder:

Westport Mob
On the night of Monday last, or morning of Tuesday, a mob broke open the store of M. McDonnell, Esq., Westport, and took

there from seven barrels of flour, which they divided amongst themselves at the door, leaving the empty barrels behind them. The watchman on the premises, whom they overpowered, could not recognise any of the plunderers.

Tyrawley Herald, 21 January 1847

The following account appears to be apocryphal, although the narrator claims that he got it from a reliable source.

SHEEP – STEALING EXTRAORDINARY

During the famine of 1847 and when nightly depredations were rife in this country, a man living in Coolcarney, a distance of three or four miles from this town, was, after a long vigilance on the part of the sufferers, caught in the act of sheep-stealing, for which he was afterwards transported. It was then considered that the neighbourhood would be free from such thefts, but soon the missing of a sheep proved the fallacy of such hopes. Sheep after sheep disappeared, and no discovery of the robber could be made. At length suspicion fell upon the wife of the convict and a sharp eye was kept upon her, when one night those on watch heard a noise close by. A sheep was gone. It could have been killed and removed by none but the sheep-stealer's wife. She was accordingly followed into her house and diligent search was made, but no sheep was found. One of the men on watch was positive and the party returned and re-examined the house but with the same fruitless result as before. The men left the house, consulted together, talked over what they had seen and heard, and once more resolved upon a closer search of the woman's house, for the missing sheep must be there. There was a charm in the third trial. The sheep was found in the bed with the children, having on a nightgown and chemise. The more tedious procedure of law was not resorted to. The woman was expelled from the neighborhood and her house thrown down. This circumstance was yesterday related to us on undoubted authority.

Ballina Chronicle, Wednesday, 2 October 1850

But not all cases that came before the courts were of such a serious nature.

According to James Daly, editor of the *Connaught Telegraph*, when giving evidence before the Devon Commission in 1843, almost all cases brought to the Petty Sessions concerned squabbles between tenants who farmed under the Rundale system of land tenure.

SIR JAMES PALMER

Sir James Palmer, Inspector-General of Prisons, carried out an inspection of the prisons in Mayo in 1835. He visited Castlebar Gaol and was pleased with what he found there. He reported to his superiors that the gaol was now one of the 'advanced scenes of Prison Discipline and Industry.'

He went on to heap praise on the governor, Thomas Gallogly:

Mr. Gallogly has very deservedly gained the confidence of the County, and we have every reason to look back with satisfaction to the decisive measures resorted to by the Grand Jury and the High Sheriff, to rescue the County from a bad system.

Gallogly had taken over as governor when the previous incumbent had to retire on health grounds. He set about introducing changes and general improvements with gusto. The Grand Jury was suitably impressed by his improvements and passed a motion commending the governor's exertions 'which reflect the highest credit upon himself and his county.'

The Archbishop of Tuam, the redoubtable John McHale, visited the prison in 1843 and wrote in the visitors' book, 'I have found so much of the best order and cleanliness that I feel pleasure in recording my approbation of the governor's attention.'

Palmer went on to add that he found the system had very much improved since his last visit but he found that there was a larger proportion of prisoners working at stone-breaking and treadmill labour than he had expected to find.

The treadmill was introduced in 1818 to provide useful employment for prisoners. It consisted of a large hollow cylinder of wood on an iron frame with steps about 7 inches apart. The criminal, steadying himself by handrails on each side, trod on these, his weight causing the mill to revolve. Resistance was obtained by weights.

Originally, these mills were used to produce something to give the prisoners a sense of purpose. In some prisons the wheel drove a mill or pumped water. The original name was 'tread wheel' but one was used to power a flour mill in Bedford prison and the term 'treadmill' evolved from its use there. But, in time, most treadmills had no purpose other than to punish.

GALLOGLY'S DOWNFALL

In 1849, Gallogly's twelve-year tenure as governor came to an abrupt and dramatic end. In the previous October, Robert Morrison, who had recently acquired The Scotch House, a drapers and haberdashers in Castlebar, was examining the account books of his predecessor. He discovered an account in the name of Thomas Gallogly for carpets, rugs, lace, silk, etc., amounting to £21. Morrison, in a written statement to the Board of Superintendence, alleged that the governor had given directions that liability for the goods be transferred to the gaol account. He accused Gallogly of 'dipping into the pockets of cesspayers for personal luxury'.

The Board of Superintendence convened and recommended that the High Sheriff dismiss the governor. In December, the sub-sheriff, named Kearney, went to the gaol and demanded possession. After some discussion and fruitless bargaining the governor handed the key of the gate over to a turnkey named Dunbar. When the sub-sheriff left, it appears that the governor had second thoughts and re-took possession of the key. The sub-sheriff returned to the gaol and again demanded the key but Gallogly refused to hand it over. The sub-sheriff left threatening to bring in the army and police. He later returned to the gaol accompanied by Lord Lucan, a member of the Board of Superintendence, and a group of constables and confronted the governor. Kearney ordered a turnkey named MacEnroe to take the key from Gallogly by force but he refused. The sergeant with the constables also refused the same request, stating that he was there to preserve the peace, not disturb it. On the direction of Lord Lucan, the sub-sheriff put his hand in Gallogly's pocket and took the key. This was in effect the governor's dismissal. The two turnkeys involved in the drama also lost their jobs that day.

PRISONERS' DIET

Males and females were kept in separate accommodation. Prisoners were classified into categories and segregated accordingly: felons, those guilty of misdemeanours, persons awaiting trial, debtors and vagrants. Breakfast for males consisted of 8oz (227g) of oatmeal and 1 pint (0.5l) of buttermilk. For dinner they were given 4lbs (1.8kg) of potatoes and 1 pint (0.5l) of new milk. Females were provided with the same menu but the portions were smaller.

AFTER GALLOGLY'S DEPARTURE

When Gallogly departed, it seems the standards of general discipline and administration dropped considerably. In his report in 1862, James Lentaigne, the inspector-general at the time, was not impressed by what he saw:

> My colleague, in his official report of Castlebar gaol in 1861, observes: — 'As in former reports, it is my unwelcome task to record the continuance of assaults as constituting the chief item of crime in this county; thus out of forty-seven males in custody, deducting debtors and lunatics, the assault cases, including that of a juvenile, fourteen years of age, amount to no less than twenty-seven!' On my inspection in July 1862, I found thirty-four males under sentences of imprisonment for assaults, showing that the lawless state of the inhabitants of this district still continues, and is rather increasing. The authorities of the gaol are anxious to do their duty, but the appliances at their disposal are very imperfect, and my experience leads me to believe that lawless, uneducated, ill-trained men, accustomed to act from impulse, the dictates of revenge, and by an appeal to brute force, can never be successfully dealt with in an associated prison; and only in separation, under a mild but firm system of prison discipline, can their rude natures be modelled into habits of order and discipline, their intelligence developed, and taught to respect the laws.

In those less enlightened times, insane people were treated as criminals and were jailed accordingly. The term 'lunatic' was applied indiscriminately to all those poor souls.

James Lentaigne had this to say on the subject in his 1862 report:

> Lunatics
> As in the other gaols of Ireland, insane patients, instead of being placed in an hospital or asylum, where their disease can be properly treated, are committed here as if they were criminals. The result must necessarily be injurious. I found on looking over the Governor's journal, which is minutely and carefully kept, that on one occasion a lunatic was found insensible in

his cell, and was only recovered by the use of restoratives, and the care of the medical officer, after treatment in the hospital; another had a cut head; but such cases must necessarily occur, and no diligence can prevent them in the anomalous position in which the insane are placed in a gaol. Fourteen lunatics were in custody on the day of my visit.

Their cases presented all the usual features which have already been described in reports on other county gaols. One death during the past year was of a lunatic.

The diet given to lunatics in this gaol is the same as that provided for other prisoners. Animal food is very seldom given to any of the inmates belonging to this class, although the necessity for animal food for the insane is universally admitted. I am anxious that the Medical Officer should understand that he has power under the Prisons Act to order them any diet which he considers their state requires.

BRIDEWELLS

Bridewells were a feature of prison life in the nineteenth century. They could be regarded as holding houses of detention where prisoners facing charges of a serious nature would be kept until their transport to the county gaol was arranged.

Petty court sessions were held in towns like Swinford, Ballinrobe and the other larger towns in the county and each had its bridewell, where those found guilty on less serious charges would be detained for short periods.

Lentaigne wasn't impressed with the general state of bridewells in the county either:

The bridewells in this county are generally very defective and wanting in the requirements for a prison, that at Belmullet particularly so.

When I visited it, ten adult prisoners were in custody, besides two children; and for their accommodation there were but three bedsteads and four beds. There was no other furniture in the bridewell, except one form. Sheets, blankets, buckets, tins, tables, forms, and chambers are much required. The locks are very insufficient, and there is no difficulty in crossing into the yard from the outside. As this building is a mere outhouse rented by the year, I would suggest that it be surrendered, and money obtained from the Consolidated Fund, interest free, under the 16th section of the Act 7 Geo. IV. Chap. 74, repayable in twenty half-yearly instalments, with which a suitable building could be erected.

EXECUTIONS

There were only three executions at Castlebar Gaol. J. Gildea was hanged in 1835 for the crime of rape. Owen Brogan suffered the same fate in 1849 for murder. The last of the three, Edward Walsh, was executed in 1873 for the murder of his wife. His sentence was carried out inside the prison as the practice of publicly hanging prisoners had been discontinued five years earlier.

Two weeks beforehand, a local photographer, Thomas J. Wynne, was allowed to take a picture of Walsh. He used this photo to advertise his business:

> With the kind permission of the Board of Superintendence and the Governor of the Mayo Prison, I have now published a most faithful VIGNETTE PHOTOGRAPH of EDWARD WALSH Hanged on the 19th August, 1873, for the MURDER OF HIS WIFE.
>
> This admirably executed Photograph was taken in the Prison two weeks previous to his Execution, and is a most accurate delineation of his character at the time. I have also a Photo of him taken about 4 years ago.
>
> Price 6d ... per post, 7d.
>
> Also a very interesting and instructive Pamphlet giving a description of his life and career from his birth to his unfortunate end.

In the second half of the nineteenth century, the numbers confined in gaols decreased. After 1857, people serving a term of penal servitude could have part of their sentences commuted through good behaviour. By 1899, there were sixteen staff and only twenty-seven prisoners in Castlebar Gaol. In 1915, the Prisons Board decided to reduce the status of the gaol. Henceforth, it would only hold prisoners on remand or those serving one week or less.

Some prisoners were briefly imprisoned there after the Easter Rising in 1916, when a number of arrests were made throughout the country.

Later it became the county headquarters of the Black and Tans and after they were recalled, the IRA tried to burn it down but was only partially successful. Finally, it was demolished in 1932, 102 years since it first opened in 1830, when the Mayo County Board of Health acquired the site for a county hospital.

Two bodies were found buried on the site when demolition work was carried out. They were almost certainly two of the three executed men. They were re-interred in the local cemetery.

3

TEN FAMOUS MAYO FACES

1. ENDA KENNY

Enda Kenny became leader of the Fine Gael party in 2002. He replaced Michael Noonan, who resigned following a disastrous general election result. Kenny got off to a good start, spending time rebuilding the party's internal structures throughout the country. The fact that the Fianna Fáil party, then in government, was becoming increasingly unpopular also helped his cause.

In 2010, he showed a hitherto unknown, steelier side to his character when a move was made to replace him with Richard Bruton, the spokesperson on finance, who was perceived to be more media-friendly.

Kenny wrong-footed the opposition, calling a meeting of the parliamentary party to vote on a motion of confidence in his leadership. To the surprise of many commentators, he won the vote and many of those involved in the heave against him were relegated to the back benches.

In the wake of his victory and the complete humiliation of his opponents, he led the party into the following election. Fine Gael and the Labour Party won a majority of seats and entered into a coalition agreement to form the new administration with Kenny as the undisputed Taoiseach.

His government had the unenviable task of leading the country through the deepest recession in the history of the state and many unpopular measures were taken. Leading up to the General Election in February 2016, there were signs that the recession had ended and that the economy was at last starting to pick up. Opinion polls suggested that the coalition would benefit from the change in the country's economic fortunes and was likely to return with a majority, albeit a much reduced one.

However, the results were inconclusive. While Enda Kenny's party, Fine Gael, remained the largest party in Dáil Éireann, the Irish parliament, its numbers have been sharply reduced. Its erstwhile coalition partner, the Labour Party, suffered the same fate. Their combined numbers have fallen well short of an overall majority so Kenny must turn to other sources if he is to get an overall majority of votes in parliament.

At the time of writing, five weeks after the election, interparty negotiations have reached an impasse and the likelihood is that a working government will not be formed in the near future. Whether the Mayo man will lead the next administration or not is a matter for conjecture at the present time but, win or lose, Kenny will long be remembered in his native county and indeed well beyond its borders.

2. MARY ROBINSON

Mary Robinson was born in Ballina in 1944 and has had a distinguished and varied career to date.

Baptised Mary Therese Winifred Bourke, she is the daughter of Aubrey Bourke from Ballina and Tessa O'Donnell from Carndonagh in Donegal. Both parents were medical doctors.

At various stages of her career, she has been a lawyer, a politician, President of Ireland (1990–97) and the United Nations High Commissioner for Human Rights.

Mary Bourke attended Mount Anville Secondary School in Dublin and afterwards, studied law at Trinity College, Dublin, King's Inns and Harvard Law School.

While still in her twenties, she was called to the Inner Bar as Senior Counsel and was appointed Reid Professor of penal legislation, constitutional and criminal law, and the law of evidence, as well as lecturer in European Community law.

In 1970, she married Nicholas Robinson, a solicitor, whom she had known since their student days. They have three children.

She served as senator in the Seanad, for the Trinity College constituency, for a period of twenty years (1969–89) and also acted as whip for the Labour Party. She resigned from that party over the Anglo-Irish Agreement of 1985, which she felt ignored unionist concerns. She was also a member of the Dublin City Council and unsuccessfully contested the general elections of 1977 and 1981 as a candidate for the Labour Party. For many years Robinson also worked as legal advisor for the Campaign for Homosexual Law Reform with future Trinity College senator David Norris.

Nominated by the Labour Party and supported by the Green Party and the Workers' Party, Robinson contested the Irish presidency election in 1990 and was successful in her bid, becoming the first woman to hold that post.

As President, Robinson adopted a much higher profile than any of her predecessors. She was outspoken on matters relating to human rights. She was the first head of state to visit Somalia after it suffered from civil war and famine in 1992 and also the first to visit Rwanda after the genocide in that country in 1994. Shortly before she stepped down as president, she took up the post of United Nations High Commissioner for Human Rights (UNHCHR).

Mary Robinson has led a long, varied and distinguished career by any standard.

3. AGNES MORROGH-BERNARD

Agnes Morrogh-Bernard was a truly remarkable individual. Where others saw obstacles she saw opportunities. She was born in Cheltenham, Gloucestershire, England, in 1842.

Soon after she was born, Agnes and her mother went to live in Cork, where the Morroghs were a prominent Catholic family.

Her grandfather Edward Morrogh had married Martha Bernard of the County Kerry landowning family and her father changed the family name to Morrogh-Bernard when he inherited his mother's family property of 7,000 acres (2,833 hectares).

By all accounts, he was a humane landlord and he looked after his tenants by providing work for the women on his lands. It was here that Agnes learned that people must be allowed the dignity of earning their own living. This experience was what inspired her devotion to helping the poor.

She realised that she wanted to spend her life in a religious order. She went to Paris in 1858 to complete her education. By the time she returned home in 1860, she had already decided she wanted to become a nun.

She entered the novitiate of the Sisters of Charity shortly after her twenty-first birthday. This order had been founded by Mother Mary Aikenhead in 1815. It was the order's mission to reach out to people in need and to help them better their wretched condition in every way possible.

She spent six months as a postulant and after a two-year testing period she was professed on 16 January 1866.

Shortly after that, she was given a teaching post in Gardener Street School in Dublin. In October 1869, Agnes suffered a serious illness and, after a period of convalescence, she worked for a short while in a convent in Donnybrook. In April 1877, under her religious name of Mother Arsenius, she arrived in Ballaghadereen, County Mayo, to become head of a new convent there.

She worked hard helping the poor and established a spinning and weaving business in that town. During her years in Ballaghadereen she realised that Foxford needed a convent to help combat poverty in the area and so, in December 1890, Mother Morrogh-Bernard and one sister went to live in Foxford.

After her arrival, she decided that a spinning and weaving business would be of huge benefit to this poverty-stricken region and duly set about achieving her ambition. Acting on the advice of Michael Davitt, the founder of the Land League, she contacted the owner of Caledon Mills in County Tyrone, John Charles Smith. Although a Protestant and a Freemason to boot, Smith agreed to help her in any way he could. He arranged for workers from Foxford to come to his business in Tyrone, where they were trained, and he loaned her his experienced trainee manager, Peter Sherry. After his arrival, Mr Sherry decided to stay. He took over the management of the fledgling factory and never went back to Caledon Mills.

With his guidance, business got underway and now the resourceful nun had to look for funds to make her dream a reality.

She convinced the Mother General of her order to give her £5,000, a substantial amount in those days, and managed to get the newly formed Congested Districts Board to advance a loan of £7,000 at a very favourable rate of interest. Remarkably, the Providence Woollen Mills, to use its business title, was up and running in just over a year since her arrival in Foxford.

In 1987, the mills went into receivership because of a downturn in demand for its products. It appeared that the strong link with its past and with the remarkable woman who established it were sundered. However, the famous old mills refused to die and re-opened in 2007 under new management and with its equipment modernised. Today it is in full production once more.

Incidentally, it must be said that Agnes did not confine her mission to improve the wretched conditions of her neighbours to the mills alone. She was instrumental in the formation of the Brass and Reed Band that is still active and well known throughout the county. The handball alley, built in 1901, is another monument to her determination not to let obstacles divert her from her course.

A remarkable woman in so many ways, she will be long remembered by the people of Foxford.

4. SHAUN NA SOGGARTH

Irish history over the last 300 years has produced no character more universally hated and execrated in the west of Ireland than the man known as Seán na Sagart (often phonetically spelt as Shaun na Soggarth). His real name was John Mullowney. In modern times this would be Maloney.

Despite his notoriety, comparatively little is known of his early life. This may be due in part to the fact that children were forbidden to mention his name and grown-up people blessed themselves or muttered an imprecation, or maybe both. When young aspirants were being recruited prior to finishing their education for the priesthood on the Continent, no candidate with the surname of Mullowney would be accepted.

England's Penal Laws against Irish Catholics got into their stride at the close of the seventeenth century and grew progressively more severe over the eighteenth century. The Oath of Abjuration was introduced in 1712 and stipulated that all Roman Catholic clergymen who did not swear to abjure all Roman Catholic practices and rituals by a certain date were to be transported and any who returned would have rendered his life forfeit to the Crown. Later in the same year, the Protestant Archbishop of Tuam, Archbishop Vesey, convened a meeting of priest hunters from all over Ireland for what would today be termed a pep talk.

Shaun Mullowney is believed to have been given a post of responsibility in this fight for the 'cause'. From that time on, he covered all of Connacht, accompanied by a posse of soldiers to protect and assist him in his priest-hunting activities. Prior to this, his patron and paymaster was Bingham of Newbrook, Claremorris. This Bingham was Lord Clanmorris while the Castlebar Bingham was Lord Lucan. Both worthies were kinsmen and were equally oppressive in their attitudes towards the ordinary people. The Brownes, who succeeded the Binghams, carried on in the same tradition. Shaun Mullowney is believed to have been born in Skehanagh, a townland 5 or 6 miles (8–9.5km) from Castlebar around the year 1680.

He was born in a turbulent part of County Mayo, an area that had been unsettled for centuries. The nearby castle of Kinturk, with its projecting hanging stone, was a place where rough justice was dispensed for centuries by the warlike Stauntons. In 1388, Edmund de Burgo (Burke), a son of the Red Earl, was drowned in Lough Mask with a stone around his neck. For their part or suspected part in his murder, the powerful de Burgos exacted a heavy revenge on the Stauntons. One sept of the Stuantons to escape the De Burgo vendetta changed their surname to Mac Evilly. This surname, formerly pronounced Mac Aveeley, is still found in the Castlebar area. Archbishop Mac Aveeley was a successor to Archbishop McHale in the See of Tuam. He is chiefly remembered for his long reign. Captain Seamas McEvilly was one of the Castlebar IRA men who died fighting the Black and Tans at Kilmeena in the long hot summer of 1921.

Shaun Mullowney was described as being powerfully built and athletic with low cunning and intuition to suit his nefarious occupation. For a long time, he seemed to lead a charmed life. When his archenemy Fergus McCormack, who fought at Aughrim as a youth and was known as the Rapparee, and others planned ambushes for him, he changed routes and plans at the last minute.

Shaun Mullowney's first murder of a priest is believed to have been that of Father Higgins at the cave of Pollathackeen on the west Mayo coast. The priest was saying Mass when Mullowney surprised him. He had almost escaped in a boat but Mullowney plunged waist deep into the water and shot him. Around 1724, a young curate, Fr David Burke, had arranged to celebrate Mass in the 'Lane' in Castlebar. Castlebar at that time was described as containing a maze of lanes.

It was a big market day in the town and the priest in disguise had been acting as an assistant to a packman or second-hand clothes dealer in his stall on the market square. The man, known as Johnny McCann, was deeply distrusted by the priest hunter.

Mullowney had a close watch kept on him in his stall. When the time came to celebrate Mass in the granary on the Lane, McCann's assistant slipped away silently to the Lane. The direction he took was noted by Mullowney, who followed slowly behind him. He saw one or two entering the granary, which was filled to the door. A lookout shouted, 'Shaun na Soggarth', several times. The crowd upstairs in the granary panicked and rushed for the door. In their mad rush, the rotten floor of the granary collapsed and one feeble old man was crushed to death.

The priest hastily stowed his sacred vessels inside his coat and jumped out the window, whereupon he was grabbed by the wily Mullowney, who had been expecting this.

As Mullowney pinned the priest down, some of the crowd pulled the priest hunter's long overcoat over his head and loosened his grip on his adversary, who lost no time in getting out of the town.

Mullowney had been responsible for having this priest transported to the Continent some years before this and he swore that he would not rest until he had the priest 'at the end of his dagger'. When all his plans and inquiries failed to yield any results, he decided to use his sister, a widow named Nancy Loughnan, as a pawn to achieve his bloodthirsty ambition.

His sister, a devout Catholic, detested Shaun and his actions but one cold, wet evening he stumbled into her cabin in Ballyheane feigning a wracking cough and weakness and asked to be allowed to stay for the night. His sister took pity on him. The following day he said he was much worse and professed repentance for his past life, saying he would die happy if he could only confess his sins to the man he had wronged so much, Fr Kilger.

Falling for this agonised plea, she went to the house of one of her neighbours, where she knew she would find both Fr Kilger and his nephew, Fr Burke. Returning with Fr Kilger, she waited outside the door and priest entered. Hearing shouts and the sounds of a struggle, Nancy entered the house and met Shaun rushing out with his bloodstained dagger. He ran across the fields towards Castlebar. Fr Kilger lay dying on the floor in a pool of blood. The widow fainted with shock.

When she recovered, she crept back to the house she had visited, as she was too weak to walk. There she told her story and fainted again. Fr Burke refused to heed her advice to flee and said he would attend the funeral and bless his uncle's grave. The funeral was hastily arranged for the following morning to hoodwink the authorities. Nevertheless, John Bingham had sent out a troop of soldiers to frighten the peasantry.

After the funeral had covered a mile or more of the road to Ballintubber, Shaun na Soggarth, who was concealed behind a whitethorn hedge, leaped out onto the road and grabbed Fr Burke, who was disguised in a long peasant's frieze coat. The priest managed to struggle free and leap over the roadside fence and run away in the direction of the Partry Hills. The epic chase with Mullowney is still remembered to this day, almost 300 years later.

The chase, which ended in Partry, covered several townlands and took a circuitous route through Dereendaffderg and Shraigh. The whole concourse, including soldiers, stood and watched until the chase disappeared from view. They might have thought the priest hunter would be happier to kill or take back his quarry singlehandedly.

The spectators saw another man suddenly joining the race and closing on the other pair. When the chase got to Partry, Fr Burke swung around in desperation and grappled with Mullowney. As both rolled on the ground, he wounded Shaun in the arm with a dagger thrust. The third runner reached them just then and lost no time in plunging his dagger into Mullowney's side. Mullowney was able to identify him as Johnny McCann.

To rub salt into the dying priest hunter's wounds, the packman told him that his name was not McCann but Higgins. 'I am a nephew of the man you murdered at Pollathackeen. I have longed and waited for the day I would avenge my uncle's death.'

Ironically, Shaun na Soggarth was buried in the cemetery of Ballin-tubber Abbey. An ash tree once marked the grave where he lay. A plain stone near Partry Garda Station is said to mark the spot where he met his death.

The two men involved in the death of Shaun na Soggarth escaped the manhunt that followed. In a party that included Mullowney's sister and McCormack, the Rapparee, they were believed to have escaped to France.

5. MARTIN SHERIDAN

Sheridan was without question the greatest athlete this country has ever known. Athletic officials and authorities on sport have given to the departed this honour ungrudgingly.

This notice appeared in the obituary columns of *The New York Times* on Sunday, 31 March 1918.

By any standards it was an extraordinary tribute. However, few, if any, who knew him would find issue with that assessment of his life and sporting career. Martin James Sheridan from Bohola, County Mayo, was indeed an extraordinary man.

He was born on 28 March 1881, in Treenduff, Bohola, about 5 miles (8km) from Foxford. He showed athletic prowess from an early age and he was able to win any local athletic event within his own age group when he was growing up.

According to *The Martin Sheridan Story*, published about twenty years ago, he is said to have developed his love for running when he was quite young and worked with his father and his brothers saving turf in Barleyhill bog, about 2 miles (3km) from his home.

His mother would signal when dinner was ready by hoisting a white flag that could be seen by her family. It was the signal for all the children to stop working and to race homewards across country in their bare feet, jumping ditches and hedges along the way.

Like so many others, he was forced to leave home in search of work when he was 19; he headed for the United States. His older brother, Richard, who was also a fine athletic all-rounder, was already there. He had left home some years previously and now worked in the police force, the NYPD. Martin followed suit.

He devoted much of his spare time to athletics in general and discus-throwing in particular. He was less than a year in the police force in New York when he broke the existing world record for discus throwing. In fact, he was never beaten in any discus-throwing event he entered before he retired from the sport a decade later.

He won the discus event in the American Championships in June 1904 and was selected to represent the US in the Olympic Games in St Louis the following September. There, he won his favourite event, setting a new Olympic record for the discus. Incidentally, he became the first Mayo person to win an Olympic medal.

Before that year was out, he won the Canadian Discus Championship and came second in the shot put and high jump competitions.

The following year, he continued on his winning way, retaining his Canadian discus title and winning the American All-Round Championship, a multi-sport event with ten disciplines.

At the Intercalated Olympics in Athens in 1906, he won the discus event and set a new world record in the process. The following day he won another gold medal when he was victorious in the 16lbs (7kg) shot competition. He also won three silver medals in three different jumping events: the standing long jump, the standing high jump and stone throwing.

On his return to New York, sports writers acclaimed him as the greatest track-and-field athlete of all time. He was also successful in his police work and was promoted to the rank of first-grade detective.

He died in St Vincent's Hospital in Manhattan, New York, the day before his 37th birthday, a casualty of the 1918 flu pandemic.

On 2 December 1988 he was inducted into the USA National Track and Field Hall of Fame in Indianapolis, the first Irish person in history to be included in this prestigious institute.

---

6. MARGARET BURKE SHERIDAN

Margaret Burke Sheridan was an Irish opera singer. Born in Castlebar in 1889, 'Maggie from Mayo', as she was known, was, arguably, Ireland's leading prima donna.

Her parents died when she was only 4 years old and Castlebar's parish priest, Canon Lyons, arranged for her to attend school in the Dominican convent on Eccles Street in Dublin.

While there, she studied music under Mother Clement, a noted music teacher, and she showed that she had exceptional musical talent. After winning a gold medal at the 1908 Feis Ceoil in Dublin, a fundraising concert was staged for her and, with the proceeds, she was sent to the Royal Academy of Music in London.

Here she met the Italian inventor, Guglielmo Marconi, who invited her to continue her musical career in Italy and arranged for her to go there. With Marconi, she travelled to Rome, where she auditioned in 1916 for Alfredo Martino, a prominent singing teacher attached to the Teatro Costanzi. After hearing her sing for the first time, Martini is alleged to have told her, 'You have a wonderful voice but you don't know the first thing about singing!'

However, Margaret worked hard to overcome this drawback and within two years, she made her operatic debut in Rome. Critics and the public alike were ecstatic and she became a celebrity overnight. Arturo Toscanini, the renowned conductor, invited her to sing Mimi in *La Bohème*. Again, she was an outstanding success and her performance here led to a series of appearances in operas by Puccini.

In 1919, she appeared for the first time in Covent Gardens, London, in the title role of *Madame Butterfly*.

She returned to Italy and over the next sixteen years she continued to captivate audiences with her performances in operas by Puccini, Mascagni, Respighi and other composers. The future Pope Pius XI, then Archbishop of Milan, said, 'Heaven came very near when I heard her singing.'

When he became Pope he offered her the title countess but she was too modest to accept the honour. La Margherita Sheridan, as she was known in Italy, never forgot her Irish connections. She always asserted that she was Irish and proud of that fact.

When the Lord Mayor of Cork, Terence McSwiney, died on hunger strike in 1920, the opera house in Naples had to close; it was announced that, 'La Sheridan will not sing; her compatriot is dead.'

She retired from singing in 1935 and returned to Dublin, where she died in 1958 and was buried in Glasnevin Cemetery. The Italian ambassador said on her death:

> She was a great friend of my country. Italy loved and admired her. She was more than a prima donna; she was literally the first great lady of the opera houses of Rome, Milan and Naples. She made us the gift not only of her golden voice but of her generous warm Irish heart. Toscanini and Puccini will ever be linked with her name.

7. MICHAEL DAVITT

Early Career

Michael Davitt was born in Straide, County Mayo, in 1846, in the midst of the Great Famine. He was the second of five children born to Martin and Catherine Davitt. When Michael was only 4, his family were evicted from their home and forced to go to the workhouse in Swinford, where Catherine discovered that rules required the family be separated. Children over 3 years of age were taken from their mothers and put in a separate section of the workhouse with all the other children. She took her family out of the workhouse and the couple decided to join many other evicted families who were emigrating to England in the hope of finding work and providing a better life for themselves and their children.

They settled in the East Lancashire town of Haslingden. Here, Michael was sent to work in a cotton mill at the tender age of 11. One day, he had his arm so badly maimed in an accident that it had to be amputated. Unable to continue working, he went back to school. He spent four years attending the local Presbyterian school and from there he acquired work as a post office clerk and printer.

He began evening classes in Irish history at the Mechanics' Institute. It was at this time that his thoughts began to turn to politics and he joined the Fenian movement in England.

Politics and Land Reform

In 1870, he was arrested for Fenian membership and firearms' offences and he was sentenced to fifteen years' penal servitude but he was released on 'ticket of leave', a form of parole, after seven years.

He was now a national figure and his release was marked by mass celebrations all over the country. He founded the Land League of Mayo along with several others, including the editor of the *Connaught Telegraph*, James Daly. He preached passive resistance to the landlord class and to every government official.

The Land League undertook a long and bitter land war against unjust rents and evictions. By 1881, the government was pressurised by the League's popularity to introduce land reform measures to pacify Irish tenants.

Davitt continued with his work of bringing about social and political change in Ireland. He was, according to the *Daily Chronicle*, 'the most impressive voice of Irish nationalism since the days of O'Connell'.

Many of his political aspirations remained unfulfilled as, to his great disappointment, the majority of those who now owned their own farms proved to be highly conservative in their attitudes and ignored his calls for political and social reforms.

He died in 1906 and was buried in his native Straide.

8. JOHN FEENEY

John Feeney, a native of Swinford, was born in 1903. When he was only 16 years old, he headed to England in search of work. He went to London and found labouring work on the roads and building sites with the building firm, McAlpine & Co.

In 1928, he decided on a change of career and set off for the United States with little money but with plenty of confidence and a fine singing voice. Someday, he promised himself, he would stand on the stage at Carnegie Hall and sing.

However, his prospects did not look good when he arrived in that country because the Great Depression had started and his type of work was hard to find. In a paradoxical way, this worked to his advantage as he had a top-quality singing voice and he decided to put this talent to use. He advertised for work as a singer and soon he was performing at diverse musical events, anything he could get paid for.

He also managed to get an extra source of income, writing a social column for the *Irish Echo*. This was in 1933, five years after his arrival in the States.

The nature of his work took him to the major venues, where he met and mingled, not only with the top artists but, more importantly, with the leading owners and promoters. Soon John himself was the star of the show. Accompanied by Paddy Killoran's orchestra, he began his singing career. He was to become the leading Irish-American tenor of his time. He performed with such names as Michael Coleman and James Morrison, both well-known Sligo fiddlers, and the Flanagan Brothers, Mike and Joe, who commanded a large and loyal following on the Irish dance-hall circuit.

John, or Jack Feeney, as he was more commonly known, quickly realised that radio was the leading form of home entertainment. His big break came when he was signed by the Shaefer Beer Company. The 'Shaefer Show' was broadcast coast-to-coast and soon the voice of John Feeney became well known and well liked throughout the land.

His repertoire included songs such as 'Mother Machree', 'Galway Bay' and 'Moonlight in Mayo'. By the musical tastes of today's Irish generation, this was mawkish and sentimental material but it suited his Irish-American following.

However, Jack Feeney didn't confine his singing to clichéd Irish dance-hall songs. He regularly packed Carnegie Hall with recitals of the classical works of Mozart, Handel and Schubert.

After a career lasting more than thirty years, he retired and returned to Ireland. Unfortunately, he didn't have much time to enjoy his free time at home. He died in 1967, following a massive heart attack, three years after his return to his native country.

9. PATRICK PEYTON, THE ROSARY PRIEST

Patrick Joseph Peyton was born in Attymass, County Mayo, on 9 January 1909. He was the sixth of nine children, four boys and five girls.

The family had a small farm on the slopes of the Ox Mountains, where life was hard for the Peyton family as the land was poor and the father, John Peyton, was an invalid. Patrick, his mother and siblings had to do most of the farm work. But his father had an inflexible rule that the rosary be said by all every night. That nightly recital was one of Patrick's most abiding memories and it spurred him on in later years to begin his worldwide campaign to get families worldwide to join together in prayer. 'The Family that prays together stays together' was his motto.

He was one of the few children who were sent to school, although his educational career was short-lived as he had to drop out in order to help with the family farm. Patrick and Thomas, his brother, decided to emigrate to America, where their sisters, Beatrice, Nellie and Mary, had already gone.

They went to Scranton, Pennsylvania, to stay with Nellie. Thomas found work in a coal mine and Patrick became sexton of nearby St Peter's church. Back in Attymass, before emigrating, he had thoughts of becoming a priest but his aspirations had to be put on hold because of family circumstances.

Now, those thoughts returned and he discussed his feelings with Monsignor Kelly, his superior. The upshot of this meeting was that he should go to high school to complete his education. This he did and he was soon joined there by his brother, Thomas. Monsignor Kelly paid for their tuition fees.

Patrick graduated from there in 1937 and decided to enter the Foreign Seminary in Washington DC. This was an institution where students prepared for foreign mission work.

However, he contracted tuberculosis in 1938 and spent a considerable amount of time in hospital. During this time, as his condition worsened, he decided to place his trust in Mary, the Mother of God. He prayed, as he had done at home, and eventually his prayers were answered and he left hospital, a cured man, in 1940.

His sojourn in hospital had cost him a year's study but, to his great surprise, a cablegram arrived from the Vatican in May 1941, giving him a special dispensation to skip the last year's preparations for the priesthood and allowing him to be ordained immediately. He was delighted with the news for it meant that he could be ordained alongside his brother.

That day, he decided to devote the rest of his life promoting the family rosary to repay Our Lady for this miraculous healing.

He decided, with the approval of his superiors, to launch a national campaign to promote the family rosary. He began to organise triduums, or religious three-day observances, all over the nation.

His crusade was supported by the American hierarchy and gained widespread support from Catholic organisations in the country. As his campaign gathered support, he used a radio station in Albany to promote his cause. He asked his listeners to join him in reciting the rosary and in this he was very successful. He moved on to use films, outdoor advertising and, later on, television to get his message across to the masses.

He was one of the first evangelists to use mass media to spread his message. Known far and wide as the 'Rosary Priest', he was one of the first truly international celebrities.

After he launched the Family Rosary Crusade in 1947, he addressed rallies in a large number of countries, including Ireland. The crowd that attended the meeting in Rio de Janeiro was estimated at 1½ million.

Father Patrick Peyton, CSC, died peacefully on 3 June 1992 in Los Angeles, California. His remains were brought to the Holy Cross Cemetery in the grounds of Stonehill College in Easton, Massachusetts, where he was buried.

He had spoken to over 30 million people during his crusades and he had reached countless millions more on radio and television shows and in film.

The Fr Peyton CSC Memorial Centre in his native Attymass was officially opened and dedicated on 10 October 1998.

10. RAFTERY THE POET

The man affectionately known to generations of Irish schoolchildren as Raifteirí an File, Raftery the Poet, was a native of Killeadan, near Kiltimagh. He was born in 1779 and was one of nine children. Anthony's father was a weaver by trade who was employed by Frank Taafe, the local landlord, so the Rafterys were somewhat better off than their neighbours. Fate dealt them a cruel blow when Anthony was eight or nine as an epidemic of smallpox swept the community and all of his siblings succumbed to the disease.

He survived but went blind; one of the last sights he saw before going blind was his eight dead siblings laid in a line on the floor. The future certainly looked grim for this blind youth as the country was in a state of deep economic depression and employment opportunities for all were few and far between. Luck for once sided with him as Frank Taafe took pity on him and employed him as a stable hand at Killeaden, his residence. Young Raftery had a natural singing voice and could play a fiddle tolerably well so Taafe had him entertain guests who called to the 'Big House'. For several years he enjoyed a stable existence and got on well with his landlord and patron and was a popular figure at wakes, weddings and other forms of entertainment in his neighbourhood.

Unfortunately for the blind musician cruel fate overtook him once more. One wild stormy night, the landlord was holding a party for a group of his cronies when he noticed that his stock of spirits was running low. In his drunken state and with no consideration for the foul weather conditions prevailing outside, he called Raftery and bade him ride to Kiltimagh and pick up a cask of whiskey from a local *síbín* or illicit public house. Raftery had no choice but to obey Taafe's command and set forth in the face of the howling gale. Along with a companion, he took the finest horse in the stable as he was under orders to return as soon as possible. But in their great haste, the boys made a mistake and the mount slipped and fell into a deep drain alongside the twisting, narrow road. The horse's neck was broken and it had to be destroyed. When Taafe heard of this mishap he was furious and banished Raftery forthwith from his estate.

Raftery had to wander the roads as an itinerant musician, often seeking help from people little better off than himself. He seems to have spent the remainder of his life plying his trade in East Galway, an area of rich farmland, where he relied on the hospitality of the local farmers to whom he was a welcome guest whenever he called by. He played music at parties and celebrations of every sort but he was also a poet of the people, composing poems which dealt with current affairs and reflected the views of the people he lived amongst. He showed commendable courage in doing so as his sentiments could have been considered seditious by the authorities. His longing for his native home never ended until his death in 1835. His most famous poem, '*Cill Aodáin*' (Killeadan) was an ode of praise of his homeland and, indirectly, of Frank Taafe, hoping Taafe would relent and allow him to return home. While the poem was extremely popular and passed into common lore around both Kiltimagh and East Galway, Taafe was offended because he felt he didn't get the fulsome praise he felt

he deserved so poor Raftery spent the rest of his life in exile. None of his poems were written down during the poet's lifetime, but they were collected from those he taught them to by Douglas Hyde, later to become the first Irish President, Lady Gregory and others, who later published them. Sever
al of his poems have been included in school curricula for many years and few if any Irish adults to the present day are unfamiliar with his gentle description of himself which begins, '*Mise Raifteirí an File*' ('I am Raftery the Poet').

> *Mise Raifteirí, an file,*
> *lán dóchais is grá*
> *le súile gan solas,*
> *le ciúineas gan crá.*
>
> *Dul siar ar m'aistear,*
> *le solas mo chroí*
> *Fann agus tuirseach,*
> *go deireadh mo shlí.*
>
> *Feach anois mé 's*
> *m'aghaidh le bhalla,*
> *Ag seinm ceoil*
> *do phocaí folamh.*

(I am Raftery, the poet, full of hope and love with eyes without light, silence without torment. Going back on my journey, by the light of my heart, weak and tired, until the end of my way.)

4

TEN FAMOUS MAYO PLACES

1. NATIONAL MUSEUM OF COUNTRY LIFE

The National Museum of Ireland – Country Life is situated in Turlough, near Castlebar, and houses the national collection of artefacts representing the Irish way of life between the 1850s and the 1950s. It is a division of the National Museum of Ireland (the others are based in Dublin)and was opened in September 2001.

Visitors to the museum can explore the traditional Irish way of life between 1850 and 1950 through objects, images and a comprehensive collection of materials gathered over more than a century of collection and categorisation. (The National Museum in Dublin was established in 1877.)

The items on display are housed in a custom-built, four-storey facility.

The collection is focused on rituals such as customs and festivals, farming and fishing, trades and crafts, domestic life and also the clothing worn by rural people during the time frame in question. Video footage and photographs are used to re-create the context in which the exhibits were used.

Apart from the archival displays, the museum deals with scholarly and educational research and conservation.

The items on display are laid out in exhibition galleries, education rooms and a conservation laboratory and there are public services as well, including a restaurant, a bookshop and a library. Displays include handcrafted harvest knots and wickerwork, spinning wheels and boats, traditional clothing, the hand-operated machinery our grandparents used and even a life-size blacksmith's forge.

The museum is located on the grounds of Turlough Park House, the ancestral home of the Fitzgerald family, landowners in the area. Part of this 'Big House' or stately home is open to the public and furnished in the style prevailing in the early 1900s.

A recent addition to the list of facilities is the Great Western Greenway's Castlebar network. It is a 6-mile (10km) trail that offers walkers, joggers and cyclists an enjoyable mix of countryside that includes fields, riverside, woodlands, quiet country back roads and urban settings and runs from the grounds of Turlough to Lough Lannagh on the western side of Castlebar town. It opened in May 2015 and by all accounts it is a very popular addition to the amenities in the area.

The museum's opening hours are:

Tuesday to Saturday
10 a.m.–5 p.m.
Sunday 2 p.m.–5 p.m.

❖❖❖

Closed Mondays (including Bank Holidays), Christmas Day and Good Friday

❖❖❖

Parents may note that baby-changing facilities are located in the disabled toilets by the Information desk in the Museum galleries. It is possible to take pushchairs/strollers around the Museum galleries, as it is fully accessible with lifts and ramps. Highchairs are available on request in the Museum café and the Museum café is a breast-feeding friendly location.

❖❖❖

Admission to the museum is free.

2. MAAMTRASNA

Maamtrasna is a remote, mountainous area in south Mayo, located between Lough Mask and Lough Nafooey, both well known for their stocks of brown trout. Maamtrasna Mountain, the centre point of the region, is the third highest mountain peak in Mayo, after Mweelrea and Nephin. It is an area of outstanding scenery and it is a popular place with anglers and hill walkers. One would have to search long and hard for a more peaceful, idyllic setting than Maamtrasna and its surrounds. Yet an event that happened there in 1882 is still remembered today and is still the cause of controversy.

On 17 August 1882, a family of five were murdered in their cottage in Maamtrasna on the Mayo/Galway border. At that time, about 250 families scratched a living from the inhospitable terrain, situated on the slopes of Maamtrasna Mountain, near the shore of Lough Mask. This was sheep-rearing country, as the poor-quality soil couldn't sustain any other form of farming. It was also very isolated and Irish was the natural language of the people. This was to be of great importance when the police carried out an investigation in the wake of the multiple murders.

Five members of the same family were in bed when they were attacked by a group of men who broke into their cottage; John Joyce, his wife Bridget, his daughter and his mother were murdered in the deadly assault and Joyce's son was so badly wounded that he died the following day as a result of his injuries. The youngest boy was attacked also but managed to survive. Another member of the family had not been at home that night.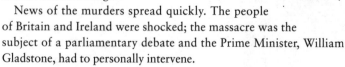

News of the murders spread quickly. The people of Britain and Ireland were shocked; the massacre was the subject of a parliamentary debate and the Prime Minister, William Gladstone, had to personally intervene.

Two days after the murders *The Times* stated that:

No ingenuity can exaggerate the brutal ferocity of a crime which spared neither the grey hairs of an aged woman nor the innocent child of 12 years who slept beside her. It is an outburst of unredeemed and inexplicable savagery before which one stands appalled, and oppressed with a painful sense of the failure of our vaunted civilisation.

To this day, the reason for this massacre is unknown though various theories have been put forward. The two surviving boys testified that the murders had been committed by a group of three or four men, with blackened faces. The authorities claimed that John Joyce was either a Ribbonman or a Fenian, both secret societies that opposed the landlords at that time, and they felt Joyce and his family were attacked because he may have stolen money belonging to one or the other of those secret, oath-bound movements.

But local rumour had it that John Joyce stole sheep from his neighbours and he and his family were victims of revenge attacks. There were others who believed that Joyce's daughter, Peggy, had a close friendship with a member of the RIC and as far as popular sentiment in the area went, he was an outright enemy of the local community.

Acting on the information of two brothers named Anthony and John Joyce (cousins of the dead man), on 20 August the police arrested ten men, all of whom resided at a considerable distance from the scene of the crime – some at a distance of 7 miles (11km). They were duly rounded up, brought before the magistrates at Cong and charged. Two of the men, allegedly from fear of execution or in expectation of reward, became informers and gave evidence against their neighbours and friends.

Although most of the men spoke only Irish, they were tried in Dublin before a judge and jury without a word of Irish. Furthermore, the presiding judge, Earl Spencer, refused to accept testimony that was written in Irish. The case was conducted in English, a language which none of the Irish-speaking accused prisoners understood.

The first three who were tried, Pat Joyce, Pat Casey and Myles Joyce, were found guilty and sentenced to death. The others decided, on the advice of a priest, to plead guilty in order to avoid the death sentence. They were sentenced to death but the judge commuted those sentenced to penal servitude for life. The three who were to be hanged were brought back to Galway Gaol. Shortly before they were executed, Patrick Casey, one of the accused, signed a declaration before the prison governor, stating that '.... as a prisoner under sentence of death ... Myles Joyce is innocent in this case'.

However, the executions went ahead.

The case was repeatedly raised in the English House of Commons. When the then Prime Minister Gladstone refused an inquiry, Charles Stewart Parnell, the leader of the Irish Parliamentary Party, withdrew his support for the Liberal government, which led to its defeat. Two of the five men convicted of the crime died in prison and the other three, two brothers and a nephew of Myles Joyce, spent twenty years in custody for a crime they did not commit.

When the men were at last released on 24 September 1902, they were put on a train from Dublin to Ballinrobe and they walked the final 18 miles (29km) home to Cappanacreha, their native village, in the darkness and the rain.

3. KNOCKNAMUCLAGH

Anyone with even a passing interest in Mayo history will have heard of the little village of Irishtown and the mass meeting held there on 20 February 1879. This event played a major part in shaping the subsequent course of Irish social history. The protest meeting was held to demand that a number of eviction notices served on tenants of the local landlord be rescinded and that an overall reduction of rent payments on this estate be implemented.

People of all sections of the nationalist community turned out in force, official estimates put the number of attendees at more than 20,000. The extremely well-organised meeting passed without a hitch and in the face of such widespread, determined opposition the landlord capitulated and not only withdrew the eviction notices but granted a 20 per cent reduction in rent to all his tenants. The positive outcome led to the formation of the Irish National Land League. The stated aim of the league was to help tenant farmers obtain control of the land they worked and to abolish landlordism in all its forms.

The following year the opportunity arose for the nascent Land League to put its policies to the test. Lord Erne, one of Ireland's many absentee landlords, owned several thousand of acres of land in the Ballinrobe region, bordering Lough Mask. Lough Mask House, the chief residence, in the little village of Knocknamuclagh, was occupied by his land agent, Charles Cunningham Boycott. The locals called him Captain Boycott. This was a term of derision because of his demeanour and air of self-importance.

As harvests had been poor that year, Lord Erne offered his landholders a 10 per cent reduction in their rents but protesting tenants demanded a 25 per cent reduction. The landlord refused to accede to this demand and Boycott then attempted to evict a number of tenants from the land.

The Land League responded by putting a policy of ostracisation into effect. Boycott soon found himself isolated – his farm workers stopped work and apart from several loyal, long-serving domestic servants and a number of young relations, Boycott was completely isolated. Local businessmen stopped trading with him; even the postman refused to deliver mail. Anyone who sided with him or supported him in any way received the same treatment.

In desperation, with the time to harvest his crops coming close, he launched a newspaper appeal for support and a number of Orangemen from counties Cavan and Monaghan volunteered their services. The story by now was being covered by newspapers around the world. The *Brooklyn Eagle* reported on 9 November 1880:

DUBLIN

Four troops of Hussars were dispatched hence for Ballinrobe by special trains at 2 o'clock this morning. Four hundred infantry have just arrived at Ballinrobe, and will encamp near Lough Mask.

These precautions are taken in view of the intention of the Northern Orangemen to send laborers to harvest the crops of Mr. Boycott, Lord Erne's agent, for whom the local peasantry, at the instigation of the Land League, refuse to work. The Government will protect a moderate force of laborers, but refuse to furnish anything approaching armed demonstrations, which would certain provoke a collision.

Boycott had stated that he needed a dozen workers but when the train carrying his new allies pulled into Claremorris rail station, he got an unpleasant surprise. Instead of the dozen or so he believed were coming to help, he found that over fifty turned up. They set off for Lough Mask House, escorted by over 1,000 policemen, and camped on the grounds. The volunteers had expected to be met by carts that would take them to Ballinrobe but they were forced to march the 14 miles from Claremorris to Knocknamuclagh, escorted by military troops, as local cart drivers refused to provide their services.

Hindered by driving rain, it was only after five hours of marching that they reached Ballinrobe where they were greeted by crowds of cat-calling, jeering, and booing locals and found little food or shelter.

Poor Boycott believed that he had serious problems while he awaited the arrival of his new friends. He soon found that his troubles magnified when they took up residence. They camped on his lawns and turned them into quagmires. His hens, duck and geese began to disappear in alarming numbers and the place soon took on the appearance of a tenement site. Feeding the multitude was a costly exercise and by the time his crops were harvested and his volunteers had been escorted back to Claremorris station, he found that the value of his crops was approximately £350 while the cost of harvesting them came to more than £10,000.

Boycott quietly decided go to England. Along with his wife and niece, he was forced to ride in an army ambulance as no local drivers would take them to the train in Claremorris. Even before his departure, his surname had passed into the English language as a synonym for ostracisation. From then onwards, many other landlords, agents and tenants who took over the holdings of people who had been evicted had the policy of boycotting used against them to great effect.

4. ROUND TOWERS

There are five round towers in County Mayo. These are early medieval stone towers of the type mainly found in Ireland, with two in Scotland and one on the Isle of Man.

Opinions differ as to their purpose; indeed, there is no reason to believe that they were all built with the same purpose in mind. The Irish term for 'round tower' is *cloigtheach*, which literally means 'bell house' and this leads many to the conclusion that they were belfries. Given their strategic location, it would be reasonable to suppose that some of them at least were built to serve as watchtowers.

The earliest towers are believed to date from the first quarter of the ninth century, and could have been built in response to the arrival of Viking marauders to this country. The first Viking raid took place in AD 795 when the monastery on Rathlin Island, off the coast of County Antrim, was plundered.

The latest ones were built in the twelfth century so, all in all, they are all between 1,100 and 900 years old.

Generally found in the vicinity of a church or monastery, the door of the tower faces the west doorway of the church.

The towers were also used as stores for foodstuffs and valuable artefacts and were used as refuges for the monks and local people when danger threatened.

Given the meaning of the Irish term for such buildings some if not all, acted as belfries; apparently the monks climbed up inside to the top floor and rang handbells out of the windows.

The towers were all built to a standard design. For such tall buildings they had very shallow foundations, some going down only about 1.5ft (0.5m) below the ground. The circumference at the base and the thickness of the circular wall varied little. Diameters, doors and windows were also designed according to a uniform plan. This suggests that most of the towers were erected by teams of builders who travelled from one monastery to another.

The five round towers in County Mayo are situated at Aughagower, Balla, Killala, Meelick, and Turlough. While there is no consensus of opinion on how or why all of them were built, it is interesting to note that all five towers in Mayo were built in the fertile limestone corridor that runs from Killala in the north to the county boundaries between Mayo and Galway.

5. THE JACKIE CLARKE MUSEUM

The museum is the most important private collection of Irish historical material in public hands, comprising over 100,000 items spanning 400 years. It includes artefacts associated with Theobald Wolfe Tone and letters from Michael Collins, Douglas Hyde, Michael Davitt and O'Donovan Rossa. It also contains rare books, proclamations, posters, political cartoons, pamphlets, handbills, works by Sir John Lavery, maps, hunger strike material and personal items from leaders of the 1916 Rising.

In 2009, the Clarke Museum opened in the old provincial bank when the collection went on display there.

Jackie Clarke (1927–2000) was an avid collector of Irish historical material since his schoolboy days. In 2005, his widow, Mrs Ann Clarke, gave his collection to Mayo County Council for the people of Ballina, Mayo and Ireland.

The exhibit is located in Ballina Town Centre on Pearse Street.

In an on-going effort to develop the collection, the walled Victorian plot has been transformed into an urban garden, which is now open to the public. The project has been realised through the support of Fáilte Ireland and the National Spatial Strategy Gateway, in conjunction with Mayo County Council, and is just the first in a series of developments that will see the entire Jackie Clarke collection made available to the public later this year.

The vast, priceless collection of historical Irish material, which was amassed by the late businessman and politician, is displayed permanently in the bank building itself. The material spans 400 years and comprises many rare and important books on the history of Ireland, and contains manuscripts, photographs, legal papers, pamphlets, handbills, newspapers (including the third edition of the *Oxford Gazette*, described as the 'first Newspaper' and dated December 1665), news-sheets, circulars, reports, autograph books and letters. The earliest item dates from 1617.

6. BALLYCROY NATIONAL PARK

Ballycroy National Park is one of Ireland's National Parks and is in the Owenduff/Nephin Mountains area of the Barony of Erris in north-west Mayo. It was established in November 1998 and it is Ireland's sixth Special Area of Conservation (SAC).

It is 11,000 hectares in size and is comprised of Atlantic blanket bog (one of the largest expanses of peat land left in Europe) and mountainous terrain, covering a vast uninhabited and unspoilt wilderness with the Nephin Beg mountain range as its central spine.

Animals to be found in the park include foxes, badgers, otters, pine martens, the invasive mink, red deer and birds like the white-fronted goose,

the skylark, the merlin, the hen harrier and the peregrine falcon.

To the west of the mountains lies the Owenduff bog. This is one of the last active blanket bog systems in Western Europe and is an important scientific and scenic feature of the National Park. The park also protects a variety of other important habitats and species. These include alpine heath, upland grassland, heath and lakes and river catchments.

The Owenduff River is also an important conservation area because it is the only river in Western Europe that drains a relatively intact and virgin blanket bog system. It is also a well-known salmon and sea trout river. There is a diversity of habitats within the National Park. On the highest peak, Slieve Carr, alpine heath is found. Other habitats include upland grassland, wet and dry heath, lakes, and the Owenduff and Tarsaghaun rivers that flow into the sea north-west of Ballycroy. However, with as much as 79 inches (2,000mm) of rainfall per year, the predominant habitat is the active Atlantic blanket bog, which covers much of the park area.

A variety of rare and interesting plants are found within this bog. These include sphagnum mosses, black bog rush (a notable component of Atlantic blanket bog), purple-moor grass, bog cotton, deer grass and cross-leaved heath.

The blanket bog contains an extensive mosaic of bog pools, which are base poor in nutrients. They are important habitats for bog bean. Other rare plants found in the park include the ivy-leaved bellflower, which flowers during July and August. This plant grows on wet grassland along the banks of the Owenduff river. Purple saxifrage, alpine meadow rue, least willow and stiff sedge, all examples of rare alpine heath plant species, have been recorded growing on the mountains in this park. These plants are more commonly found at high altitudes in colder areas of Europe. The dominant plants that are also found in the mountain areas include bell and ling heather, crowberry and bilberry.

The Ballycroy National Park Visitor Centre, located in Ballycroy village between Mulranny and Bangor, houses an interpretative exhibition of the landscape, habitats and species found in the National Park, as well as information on the surrounding area. There is a short nature trail with a viewing point, which offers great scenic views of Achill Island to the west, and the Nephin Beg mountain range to the east. Additional facilities include toilets, a coach car park, outdoor picnic areas and a coffee shop. There is disabled access to the visitor centre.

7. THE GREAT WESTERN GREENWAY

The Great Western Greenway is an off-road trail in west Mayo. It is a 26-mile (42km) stretch of a former railway line that once ran from Westport to Achill Island. Those who thought of the initiative to develop the old, disused line and replace it with a path designed for cyclists and pedestrians must have had Occam's razor in mind as they set about their work. This principle holds that where numerous solutions to a problem exist, the simplest one is generally the best.

The project has been a great success, with 400 people on average travelling the path daily, either its entire length or just sections of it. Business people along the route report a healthy upsurge in business and it is noteworthy that a large proportion of those who use it are return visitors.

Although most of the Greenway is off-road, there are a couple of sections where cyclists and pedestrians have to use the road. There are plans afoot to extend the Greenway to Castlebar as well as to Croagh Patrick.

8. KNOCK AIRPORT

Monsignor James Horan is known locally and with good reason as 'the man who built Knock Airport'. At his behest, a construction firm moved a number of large earth graders onto a hilltop in 1980, in a 'foggy boggy place', as an unimpressed government minister said, referring to the Monsignor's plans for an airport there. However, neither James Horan nor the handful of hardy souls who believed in him and his plans paid the slightest heed. Pope John Paul II had visited Ireland in 1979 and over 300,000 people had turned up at Knock when he visited the Marian Shrine and raised the status of the modern church there to basilica. Following on the papal visit, Monsignor Horan believed that Knock could become one of the major Marian sites in the world.

The construction of an international airport in the Knock region had commenced. There were many twists and turns on the road ahead but Horan did not allow obstacles of any sort stand in his way as he oversaw operations from start to finish.

He was confronted by sceptics everywhere when construction work began.

Shortly after the commencement of the project, the RTÉ reporter Jim Fahey arrived on the scene with a camera crew.

He could hardly believe his eyes when he saw the frantic activity going on around him.

'What is going on here?' he asked Horan.

'I think they are building an airport, Jim,' was the reply he received.

Fahey persisted, 'But do you have planning permission?'

'Do you know what, I can't say if we have or if we haven't,' was the monsignor's reply, delivered with his trademark hearty laugh.

Many watching the televised interview must have thought that he was simply mad but those who knew him well knew that there was nothing simple in this individual's make-up.

The project to build an airport at Knock faced many difficulties in the early days. There was one crisis after another and probably the biggest blow of all was the 1982 government decision to withhold further government funding after the initial tranche of €10 million had been paid out. Undaunted, Horan organised a massive Jumbo Draw that took in over €4 million. He got the airport finished on schedule and Charles Haughey, leader of the opposition in Dáil Éireann who officially opened it in 1986.

The monsignor was a passenger on the first flight out of Knock Airport, leading a pilgrimage to Rome but sadly, just a few months after the official opening of the airport, he died while on another pilgrimage to Lourdes.

The man may have died but his legacy endures. Knock Airport or Ireland West Airport, as it is more commonly called nowadays, had its most successful year in 2014, with over 700,000 people passing through.

While Monsignor Horan will most probably be remembered for the building of Knock Airport, it is also to his credit that he helped to develop Knock shrine and its magnificent basilica.

9. THE CÉIDE FIELDS

The Céide Fields is an archaeological site about 5 miles (8km) north-west of Ballycastle. Here, beneath the wild bog lands of north Mayo, lies the most extensive Neolithic Stone Age monument in the world. It consists of field systems, dwelling areas and megalithic tombs.

The stone-walled fields are the oldest we know of and are covered by a natural blanket bog with its own unique vegetation and wildlife. Using various dating methods, it was discovered that the creation and development of the Céide Fields goes back almost 6,000 years.

In the 1930s, a local schoolteacher, Patrick Caulfield, noticed piles of stones, which he uncovered while cutting turf in his bog. He realised two very important points – firstly, the way the stones were piled up couldn't be natural so somebody had to have put them there, and secondly, because they were underneath the peat, they had to have been put there prior to the growth of the bog itself and so must be very ancient.

Nothing of note was done about this discovery for almost another forty years until Patrick's son, Seamus, having studied archaeology, began to investigate further. It is now known that these are the remains of a Stone Age landscape of stone-walled fields, houses and megalithic tombs, well over 5,000 years old that have been preserved beneath the growing blanket bog over thousands of acres in north Mayo.

The continuing research, which involves the location and mapping of these hidden walls by probing with iron rods and the excavation of habitation sites and tombs is yielding a unique picture of the way of life of our ancestors 200 generations ago.

The first settlers to arrive in the area were farmers from mainland Europe. This site has about fifty homesteads, indicating a population of about 300 people. With the basic implements of the time, these Neolithic farmers cleared the site of trees and constructed regular field systems with stone walls. Their main economy was cattle-rearing but some of the smaller fields indicate that wheat and barley were grown there also. There are indications that the settlement included craftspeople and builders who worked in both wood and stone.

The climate at the time was much warmer, leading to almost year-round growth potential. Samples taken from the remains of trees found in the bog provide ample evidence of this. No one knows why they left the area but it seems probable that a gradual change of climate hastened their departure.

Those who left probably went no further than a few miles away from the area. There, the bog never grew and farming continued around Ballycastle. It is quite likely that some natives of north Mayo today are descendants of these first farmers.

10. THE COLONY

The first half of the nineteenth century saw an upsurge in Protestant missionary activity in Ireland. This was largely a reaction to the sense of crisis in Protestant circles following both the Act of Union of 1800, and the attainment of Catholic Emancipation in 1829. There was a strong belief amongst evangelical Protestants that if the Catholic Irish could be converted to the Protestant faith, then the problems, such as economic backwardness, lack of respect for the law, and hatred of the Protestant establishment would be eradicated.

Schools were set up to educate the children and food kitchens were established in many areas. The Catholic Church authorities, in particular the Archbishop of Tuam, John McHale, bitterly opposed what they considered underhand tactics to entice people to switch religions.

One of the leading figures of this movement was Revd Edward Nangle, who established a proselytising mission, widely known as 'The Colony', at Dugort on Achill Island in 1831. There was a church, a hospital, a kitchen, two substantial dwellings for two clergymen, a steward's house and thirty cottages in this colony.

Nangle first arrived in Achill on board a relief ship, funded by English charities, in response to one of the many famines that hit the west of Ireland in those times. He was struck by the dramatic scenery and beauty of the island and by the primitive but noble 'savagery' of the people.

He decided to found a Protestant colony there with the aim of bringing Christ and the Bible to this forgotten part of Ireland. Using funds supplied by the same charities, he rented the island of Achill from the landlord, Sir Richard O'Donnell.

He published a huge amount of propagandist tracts and pamphlets attacking 'The idolatry of Rome'. He also published a newspaper, *The Achill Missionary Herald and Western Witness.*

In his writings and sermons, he had a forceful, abrasive style for which he incurred (and enjoyed) the hostility of both Catholic and Protestant clergy. During the worst years of the famine, he was often attacked for diverting monies intended for relief to his missionary activities, which included his 'souper' policy. (Giving the starving masses soup that contained meat on Fridays, contrary to the beliefs of Catholics.)

On one occasion one of his boilers for preparing soup was hidden by 'idolaters'. Nothing daunted, Revd Nangle had small portions of raw beef doled out to his 'customers' while awaiting another boiler from Galway.

Some days later, one of his agents came across a bunch of juveniles playing a type of football game. Many of the players were barefooted and wearing the kilt-like smock, which was standard among many juveniles in rural areas in those days. The agent thought that they were kicking around a young hedgehog, or '*gráinneóg*', but when he inquired one youngster said, 'We are kicking the Devil out of the Protestant beef'. A tough-looking lump of gristle and sinews bore out his statement. The agent reckoned that their mothers were to blame. 'They cooked their share of the little cow too fast,' he said. 'Tell them to cook it slower the next time.' From that time on, local people, when they encountered very tough meat or other substance, referred to it as being 'as tough as Nangle's little cow'.

Nangle persevered and gave a good deal of temporary relief, and doubtless saved many lives. By 1853, he was reckoned to have almost one third of the teeming population of the island converted to Protestantism, despite the efforts of the Catholic Church to resist this.

In *A Tour in Connaught* (1839), Caesar Otway, a Protestant clergyman, relates a sermon preached against the mission by Fr Dwyer, parish priest of Achill Island:

Have nothing to do with these heretics — curse them, hoot at them, spit in their faces — cut the sign of the cross in the air when you meet them, as you would against devils — throw stones at them — pitch them, when you have opportunity, into the bog holes — nay more than that, do injury to yourselves in order to injure them — don't work for them, though they pay in ready money — nay, don't take any medicine from their heretic doctor [Neason Adams], rather die first.

Edward Nangle and the Protestant colony helped Achill in a very real way, despite all the lofty rhetoric and self-righteousness. In the spring of 1847, Nangle reported that the colony was giving employment to 2,192 labourers and feeding 600 children a day in the schools.

At first, Nangle distributed aid to the starving of Achill under strict conditions. Pressure was put on the recipients of food aid and work to convert to the Protestant faith. This earned Nangle the derogatory labels of 'souper' and 'Black Protestant'. As the situation worsened, and the island became totally reliant on the colony for relief, Nangle relaxed the conditions, and distributed aid freely.

In 1853, the potato crop was better than it had been for a long time. There was a repeat the following year, with the result that Nangle's converts began to return to their original religious beliefs.

Nangle later left on promotion to the rectorship of Skreen in north Sligo. He astounded his friends and critics by buying out the Achill Island estate from his former landlord, Sir Richard O'Donnell, in the Encumbered Estates' Court.

The price of £17,500 was regarded as a colossal sum for those days. (This purchase eventually led him to spending the last years of his life in violent opposition to Michael Davitt's Land League.)

By the 1880s, the Achill mission colony was dead in all but name, having submitted to the overwhelming forces ranged against it. Nangle's death in 1883 hastened its demise and an eventful chapter of Achill's history was ended.

5

GRANUAILE

Gráinne Ní Mháille (Grace O'Malley) must surely have been the most colourful character in Irish history. She was the daughter of Eoghan 'Dubhdara' Ó Máille, the leader or chieftain of the O'Malley clan at the time of her birth in or about 1530.

At that time, most of Ireland was divided into 'tuatha', small independent kingdoms, each ruled by a chieftain like Eoghan Ó Máille. A Gaelic chieftain and his Tánaiste, or next-in-line, were elected by clan members on the death of the previous leader as, under the Brehon Laws of the Irish system a chieftain had only a lifetime's interest in the clan's territory. On his death, his lands reverted to the clan, which then elected another leader.

The O'Malleys were a maritime community who lived in the area known as Umhall, beside Clew Bay. They carried on a lucrative trade with the northern ports of Spain at the time, exporting cargoes of oats, wheat and barley and returning with loads of luxury goods. Fishing and pirating were other activities of theirs and they raided and traded along the western seaboard of Ireland to the northern end of Scotland. The motto of this sea-going clan was, '*Terra Marique Potens*' (Powerful on Land and Sea).

Legend has it that her nickname, 'Granuaile' (Bald Gráinne), was bestowed on her by her father and brothers after she managed to stow away on an O'Malley ship sailing to Spain. She had begged her father to let her go there but he steadfastly refused to do so. Nothing daunted, she cut off her long, flowing tresses and dressed herself as a boy. She managed to board one of the ships and the fleet was on the high seas before anyone realised that she was a girl. Her father must have been in an indulgent mood when she returned safely because he dubbed her 'Gráinne Mhaol'.

At the age of 16, she was married to Donal O'Flaherty. Being Tánaiste to The O'Flaherty (i.e. next in line to be head of the clan), he was a good match. He was known as *Donal-an-Chogaidh* (Donal of the Battles) because of his aggressive nature.

During their marriage, Grainne bore three children, Owen, Murrough and Margaret. She gradually eclipsed her husband, actively engaging in politics, intrigue, tribal disputes, fishing and trading. The O'Flahertys were also a sea-going clan so Grainne felt at home there from the start.

The city of Galway, one of the largest trade centres in the British Isles, had closed its gates to the O'Flahertys and so they had to trade with Munster, Ulster, Scotland and Spain. However, the Corporation of Galway could not prevent her from harassing merchant ships on their way to and from Galway. She would force the ship's captain to hand over a suitable price for safe passage or allow her men to pillage and plunder his ship. The merchants in Galway complained to the English administration in Dublin but they could do nothing about it, as they didn't have the money to do anything to help.

One of the reasons why Granuaile became the effective leader of the O'Flahertys was that her husband lived up to his nickname, Donal of the Battles. He was killed during one of the interminable squabbles he had with the Joyces.

According to Brehon Law, a widow of a chieftain was entitled to a third her husband's estates but this was not handed over to Granuaile. With her two sons grown and trying to secure their own place, she returned to Umhal with 200 followers, many of whom had been her husband's men. She set up her base on Clare Island in Clew Bay. In this ideal setting she could monitor virtually all the ship traffic going along the coast. Between piracy, charging for safe passage and providing pilots for strangers to the western seaboard, she did very well for herself and her followers.

Furthermore, as her father grew old, she assumed effective leadership of the O'Malley clan, so she became a force to be reckoned with from Scotland to Spain and Portugal. English authorities in Dublin reported to the English Crown that 'she was the most notorious woman in all the coasts of Ireland'.

She once rescued a young man named Hugh de Lacy in the teeth of a gale when his ship was wrecked on Achill Island. She fell madly in love with him but her joy soon turned to sorrow when her lover was killed by a neighbouring clan, the McMahons from Erris. She bided her time until she was able to catch them unawares and then she exacted revenge for her lover's death by personally killing those responsible for his murder. Granuaile was definitely not a person to be trifled with.

In 1558, Elizabeth I succeeded to the throne of England. She was determined to bring all of Ireland under her rule; however, like her father Henry VIII, she hadn't the resources to fund an army but she had other ideas. Whereas those who observed Brehon Law in Ireland elected a new leader when the leader of a clan died, the English observed the practice of primogeniture. That meant, in effect, that the property of any noble passed, on his death, to his first-born son when he died so there was never any doubt about his successor. In theory, the Gaelic practice of selecting a new leader should have seen the most able candidate taking charge but this seldom worked in practice; few, if any, who got elected as chieftain got the full support of the entire clan. There were always sore losers and the English took advantage of this.

Elizabeth offered English titles to any Gaelic leader who agreed to accept her authority. This led to division amongst the Gaelic clans as anyone who accepted an English title would try to ensure that his eldest son took over when he died while others in the clan would seek to have the new chieftain elected in the traditional manner.

Primogeniture ensured that English influence in all parts of Gaelic Ireland was increasing all the time as the number of Gaelic chieftains who decided to accept Elizabeth's authority increased, slowly but surely. Meanwhile, Granuaile held sway over the western seas from her base on Clare Island.

In a political move, Grace married her second husband, Richard Burke, in an effort to strengthen her hold on the west coast areas of Ireland. Since the death of Donal, she had built her empire to include five castles and several islands in Clew Bay, but needed Carrigahowley Castle on the north-east side of the bay to complete her stranglehold on the area. Richard Burke owned a number of castles in the Burrishoole area, including the one at Carrigahowley that Granuaile coveted.

Legend has it that Gráinne travelled to the castle when Richard was there, knocked on the door and proposed marriage to him. Apparently, he accepted her offer.

As Brehon Law allowed divorce, she said they should marry for a period of one year and then review their relationship. One year after their marriage, Richard returned to Carrigahowley Castle after another plundering spree. He found the door locked and Granuaile standing on the battlements. She is said to have called out, 'I release you', which under Brehon Law released him from his marital obligations and allowed him to decide if he wished to end their marriage or to continue the relationship. Apparently, he turned down her offer as they remained together until his death, seventeen years later. They had a son, Tiobáid or Theobold.

Tradition has it that Theobald was born on the high seas while Gráinne was returning from a trading mission. The day after the birth they were attacked by Turkish pirates. The captain informed her that the battle was going against them. She stormed onto the deck and shot the first Turk she saw. Her crew rallied. They captured the ship, dispatched its crew and added it to their fleet.

But times were beginning to change. Many Irish chieftains had submitted to the English throne. In March 1576, The O'Malley (not her father, who had previously died) was summoned to give his submission in Galway to Sir Henry Sidney, the Lord Lieutenant. Sometime in 1577, Gráinne presented herself to Sidney and submitted.

He wrote:

> There came to me also a most famous feminine sea captain called Grany Imallye, and offered her services unto me, wheresoever I would command her, with three galleys and 200 fighting men, either in Scotland or Ireland; she brought with her, her husband for she was as well by sea as by land well more than Mrs. Mate with him; he was of the Nether Burkes and now as I hear Mack William Euter, and called by nickname Richard in Iron. This was a notorious woman in all the coasts of Ireland.

In Ireland at the time it was a matter of survival at all costs. If giving a promise of good behaviour to the English was the best option to take then it was done. Her husband, according to Brehon Law, was next in line for The MacWilliamship but the present holder had submitted and agreed to enforce English law, including that of primogeniture. Establishing good relations was all the more important to secure her husband's future.

Sir Philip Sidney had accompanied Sir Henry, his father, and apparently was quite taken with Gráinne. He corresponded at length about her but most of this correspondence has been lost. One story does relate how Sir Henry asked her to conduct him and his entourage around the bay to view the city's harbour and defences. She did agree, but, being a businesswoman, demanded and was given payment.

The Lord Lieutenant realised that she would make a better friend than an enemy and she was able to return home and take up where she had left off, pirating and plundering as usual.

In 1577, while raiding the Earl of Desmond, she was captured for the first time. She was handed over to the President of Munster, the Lord Justice Drury, who wrote:

> Grany O'Mayle, a woman that hath impudently passed the part of womanhood and been a great spoiler, and chief commander and director of thieves and murderers at sea to spoille this province, having been apprehended by the Earle of Desmond this last year, his Lordship hath now sent her to Lymrick where she remains in safe keeping.

Later she was transferred to the dungeons of Dublin Castle, demonstrating her importance as a prisoner. Very few imprisoned there ever got out again but, by some means, Gráinne was set free to return to Connaught with a promise of good behaviour.

On 24 November 1580, The MacWilliam died. After a brief scuffle and negotiations, Gráinne's husband, Richard-an-Iaraínn, was installed and was later knighted in 1581. This put Gráinne into a new role of power and amongst the other wives at one gathering she was singled out 'among them Grany O'Malley is one and thinketh herself to be no small lady'.

On 30 April 1583, Richard died, surprisingly of natural causes. Gráinne wasted no time and 'gathered together all her own followers and with 1,000 head of cows and mares departed and became a dweller in 'Carrikahowley in Borosowle'. Having been cheated of her right to one-third of her first husband's estate she established her claim simply by taking it.

Gráinne was no stranger to danger and prized courage and valour. Her contempt for cowardice is evident in one tale of when she was fighting the Stauntons of Kinturk Castle. Apparently in the midst of battle her son Tibbot faltered and drew back to shelter behind his mother. '*An ag iarraidh dul i bhfolach ar mo thóin*' ('Is trying to hide behind my backside you are – the place you came from?'), she asked.

Thus mortified, he stood his ground and the Stauntons eventually surrendered.

VISIT TO LONDON

By 1593, the power of the English Crown had grown significantly and Gráinne had spent a number of long, difficult years struggling to keep control of her ancestral territories. The English governor of Connacht, Sir Richard Bingham, had been appointed by the Queen to bring order to the province and to quell the rebel elements that had refused to surrender their independence.

When her brother and her son were captured and imprisoned by Bingham, Gráinne petitioned the Queen directly to have them released and in return for these pardons, she undertook to defend the Queen's interests in her area on land and on sea. However, when she received no reply to her entreaties, she decided to go to London and see the Queen in person.

Amazingly, her little convoy of galleys reached London without incident and, stranger still, the Queen agreed to meet her. The meeting between these two imperious women has become the stuff of legend. Gráinne refused to bow to Elizabeth because she wanted to show that she did not regard herself as a vassal of the Queen. The courtiers were outraged but Elizabeth passed no comment. She was concerned, however, when it was discovered that Gráinne was carrying a dagger.

The meeting might have ended then, with the visitor being thrown in a dungeon, but Elizabeth seemed to accept Gráinne's explanation that the dagger was merely for her protection. There was further drama before the meeting ended. Gráinne sneezed and one of Elizabeth's ladies-in-waiting gave her a lace handkerchief. Gráinne apparently blew her nose once and then tossed the handkerchief into the open fire. The court was outraged that the ungrateful guest had thrown away such an expensive gift. Gráinne insisted that in Ireland, a used handkerchief was considered dirty and no one of breeding would keep it to use a second time. It seemed that Gráinne was deliberately going out of her way to shock in order to show that she would not be intimidated by Elizabeth and her English courtiers.

Both ladies conversed in Latin and apparently got on quite well because the Queen agreed to her requests and decreed that Bingham should release the captives.

A NEW ORDER

Gráinne was known as a fearless leader and a fierce fighter. In her seventy years of life, she and her family saw the English rule spreading throughout Ireland and she was the last Gaelic leader to succumb to the new order.

Her son, Tiobóid Bourke, was a man who changed sides as he saw fit several times in his career. He was eventually rewarded with the new title of Viscount Mayo. He met his death while attending a pattern or festival at Ballintubber Abbey in 1629 when, during the festivities, he insulted one of his kinsmen and paid the ultimate price.

The Gaelic people were very fond of a variation of the sport of leapfrogging and a competition was held during the pattern celebrations. Tiobóíd decided to take part, no doubt well inebriated at the time. Being well over 60 years of age and considerably overweight, he looked around for someone smaller than he was to be his partner. He picked on a kinsman, Diarmuid Burke, who was known as *Diarmeen Cruchtach* (Little Hunchbacked Dermot).

Diarmeen felt his kinsman was mocking him because of his disability and decided to take his revenge. He concealed a short knife in his leather jerkin and as Tiobóid leaped over him, he stabbed upward with his dagger and killed him. Tiobóid-na-Loing was buried within the precincts of Ballintubber Abbey.

6

RELIGION AND SUPERSTITION

OUR ANCESTORS' BELIEFS

The faith of the Irish people since Christianity took hold until relatively recently was a mixture of pre-Christian practices, animism and Druidism, with a veneer of Christianity.

Mayo people, being on the periphery in so many ways, were slower than most other parts of the country to abandon the old customs, beliefs and superstitions. According to the folk historian John Henry, many old people in the Swinford area, as late as the late 1950s, still believed in the existence of fairies who interacted with mortals. They believed that the '*Féar Gortach*' was still to be found in many places. The *Féar Gortach* or Hungry Grass was supposed to be patches of cursed grass. Those foolhardy enough to walk on this grass were immediately struck by pangs of temporary hunger and would lose their sense of direction, walking around in circles until they dropped to the ground out of sheer exhaustion.

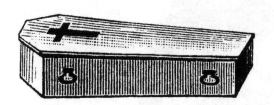

The only effective antidote was to immediately remove one's coat or outer garment and turn it inside out before putting it back on again, while reciting a prayer for deliverance to the Blessed Trinity. Sometimes a particular saint would be added to the list as well. Some of the elders of Henry's generation believed that carrying a slice of bread or a potato to eat when hunger struck was a great help also.

There were various reasons given to him to explain the existence of the affected grass but in all of them the death of some unshriven individual was somehow involved. Many said that *Féar Gortach* grew at the spot where the coffin of someone who had died during the Great Famine was put down so the bearers could have some rest. Others felt it marked the spot where someone met a violent and unexpected death, without an opportunity to shrive, or go to confession and receive absolution.

CHANGELINGS

The common people believed in changelings. That meant the abduction of a healthy child by the fairies, who replaced him or her with a weak, sick substitute. Some said the substitute was a '*síóg*', a fairy on the point of death. For countless generations, the common folk believed that fairies were malevolent beings, always ready to interfere in the business of mortal beings and usually for some maleficent reason.

Furthermore, the belief that children, especially boys, were always at risk was widespread. Therefore, boys were often dressed as girls when going away from their home to minimise the risk of them being kidnapped. This practice lasted until well into the twentieth century.

THE FAIR PEOPLE (*AOS SÍ*)

The Church, up to the middle of the last century at least, was never able to completely replace the Druid with the priest. A concerted attempt was made to replace pre-Christian festivals and sacred places with Christian equivalents but with mixed results.

Pre-Christian events, such as the festivals of Samhain and Bealtaine, still went ahead but they had name changes and attempts were made to remove the pagan elements of the rituals and to replace them with Christian practices and beliefs.

Up until the late 1960s, bonfires were lit at crossroads and other gathering places on St John's Eve, 23 June, the longest day of the year. Nominally, the celebrations that accompany the lighting of the fire took place on the eve of St John's Day. However, the lighting of bonfires and the games and customs that accompanied them had been part of pagan rituals to celebrate the summer solstice and pre-dated the feast of St John by centuries.

It was a classic case of the Church attempting to give a pagan feast a Christian makeover. Some customs observed on that night were not of pagan origin. No one was allowed to dance on that night on account of the girl who had danced in front of St John the Baptist on the night he was executed. Also, rosary beads, scapulars, and other pious objects, which had become worn or had been broken, could be cast into the bonfire without the risk of divine retribution.

Samhain, marking the end of the bountiful harvest season and the onset of winter, the 'dark' part of the year, was a major Druidic festival. Feasts were prepared and the souls of dead relations were asked to attend and to partake of the meal.

Samhain was a time when the '*Aos Sí*' or fairies that lived in underground caverns could move about in our world. Mayo is dotted with Iron Age ringforts and many believed that fairies lived underneath many of them, so people in general were loath to interfere in any way with those forts because of fear of retribution from the fairy folk. There are many that have remained untouched since Iron Age farmers first built their houses on them.

There are many trees to be found throughout the county that were, and still are to some extent, regarded as belonging in some way to the fairies. Anyone foolish enough to cut down or to interfere with one in any way could expect trouble. He or she could expect to find thorns in their beds when they retired at night and would be unable to get a wink of sleep and this could go on indefinitely. Picking the thorns out of the bed wasn't a solution either because they would mysteriously re-appear when the unlucky person went to bed the next night.

Fairies were thought to be ever-present in the midst of mortals, going about their normal routine.

Generally, they didn't interfere unless they were provoked and then their retribution could be severe and immediate. A person might fall and break a leg or a cow or horse might take ill and die, and for many, this would be the result of a fairy curse. Anyone throwing dirty water out over the half door had to shout 'hurrish' in a loud voice before doing so. The danger was that some fairy might be passing by and would be less than happy if it was deluged with a bucket of dirty water!

As there was a strong, almost universal belief that fairies had good hearing, accompanied by quick tempers, every effort was made to placate them and they were always referred to in the politest possible manner. Hence, terms like the 'good people' or the 'fair folk' were used when people spoke aloud about them.

Otherwise, an eavesdropping fairy might take exception to something that was said about his people and the unfortunate individual who uttered the offensive remark might find that the butter wouldn't 'come' the next time a churning was done in his or her house.

THE DEVIL

But fairies were not the only non-mortal beings the Irish common folk had to contend with. It was widely believed that the Devil and his associates were continually on the prowl, looking for souls to snare and take down to Hell.

The Devil was still a force to be reckoned with in the Mayo of the 1950s and there were various charms and prayers to keep him at bay. If this malevolent entity was encountered, and he could well be abroad, especially during the hours of darkness, the standard defence was to call on the Father, Son and Holy Ghost in a loud clear voice to send him back to where he came from. The person in question made the sign of the cross at the same time.

Many stories were told of instances when a priest was called to visit some person who was in danger of death and the Devil tried hard to prevent this from happening. John Henry related the story of a monk from Ballinsmall Abbey, near Claremorris, who was hurrying along the Claremorris–Knock road one night, responding to a sick call from a parishioner who was at death's door. He was accompanied by a neighbour, Mark Forkan, who carried a military-style lantern to light their way, a novelty in those days as the only torches used by peasants were burning coals impaled on iron spikes or old reaping hooks.

They were passing a well-known shebeen, or illegal pub, when the lantern holder noticed two unusually shiny gold coins lying on the ground. Forkan thought that they should use the coins to get a tumbler or two of punch to help them on their way. In those days, the steaming bowl of whiskey punch was a popular remedy among the peasantry for most human ills. Nearly everybody had faith in a bowl of punch in its own good time, and in this regard the friar was no exception.

He hesitated but only for a moment. He then bade his man to cover the crowns with two small flagstones from the road fence. 'If they are there on our return, well and good', he said. The friar arrived at his

destination just in time, and with not a minute to spare, to anoint a young man who lay dying.

On their return along the road, the pair decided to retrieve the coins they had placed under the flagstones. All they found was a large '*ciaróg*' or beetle under each stone.

There are many variants of this tale to be found in different parts of the county but all have one thing in common. The priest is the hero in each version and the devil is thwarted in his attempts to snare the soul of a dying person by preventing the priest from administering the Last Rites.

OLD ANIMAL CHARMS AND CURES

Two miles west of Bohola along the main road to Castlebar lies the townland of Loughkeeraun. The tiny bogland lough or lake from which the townland got its name has completely disappeared over the past half century owing to local drainage operations. There was an old tradition that St Kieran cured a valuable cow that was dying with water taken from the loch and because of this the loch was a popular place of pilgrimage for centuries.

Pilgrims came to Loch Kieran mainly to pray for luck and prosperity with their livestock in the forthcoming year. Not to be outdone in religious fervour or whatever, some pilgrims took rolls of butter to throw into the lake as an offering to the saint.

More practical local people came later and salvaged the rolls of butter. Having recycled the butter, it was packed into their butter firkins and sold in the Swinford butter market. I can remember pilgrims going to Loch Kieran on 15 August, which seemed to be the most popular date of all for local pilgrimages in this country.

For a kicking cow, a popular cure was to get two people to pass a burning sod of turf under and over the standing cow in the names of Saints Patrick, Bridget and Colmcille. For a newly calved heifer cow to give butter-rich milk, a similar ritual was performed. In this case, the lighted turf sod was passed around the cow's hind legs in the names of the Blessed Trinity.

I can remember on one occasion, while assisting an aunt in this operation, the cow showed her disapproval by kicking the burning sod into a bundle of straw, almost setting fire to the byre. Having been rebuked for laughing, I was told that the fire was blessed. However, I felt that the ritual was more of pagan than Christian origin. In some districts down to the present day, giving away milk on May Day was forbidden as it was regarded as giving away one's luck for the rest of the year. Giving away fire on that day was also taboo. I recall a story by an old neighbouring woman who absentmindedly went to borrow a coal on May morning when she found her fire had gone out. Her return trip was done in record time without the coal of fire.

In bygone times, beef and butter were the most important items in rural economy – as they are at the present time. Anybody found trespassing on a neighbour's land on May Day might be suspected of gathering certain lucky herbs in order to take the neighbour's luck. If the trespasser could be heard saying the words '*Im agus bainne dom*' (Milk and butter to me) when plucking herbs on another man's land, he was in real danger.

The use of the dead hand to bring luck in butter gathering is happily a thing of the past. The last known instance of anything in that line being practised in Mayo was over 100 years ago at a point where the three parishes of Killedan, Knock and Kilcolman join, almost midway between Claremorris, Kiltimagh and Knock. An old woman who lived alone was being waked in the year 1850. A frightening thunderstorm sprang up during the night that so frightened all at the wake that they all rushed out and away home.

When some of them returned the following morning, they found that the old woman's right hand had been severed and taken away. I heard this tale being told by an old man, John Hynes, over fifty years ago. His father was one of those who attended the old woman's wake. In some cases, animal help was invoked to cure human ailments. Donkey's milk and ferret's leavings (food), together with the fasting spit and boiled primroses, were time-honoured cures for jaundice and other mystery complaints. Some of those confirm the saying of the cure being worse than the ailment.

John Henry, *Folktales from County Mayo*

THE ROLE OF THE PRIEST IN IRISH SOCIETY

From the earliest Christian times, priests were held in high regard by all. Priests said Mass and administered the sacraments and carried out all the conventional duties of their office and they were held in awe by their flocks. Many clergymen used their power and status in the community for the betterment of their flocks while others, simply put, used them to suit their own ends.

Countless cases are reported of priests 'inviting' some of the better-off members of their congregations to rear a couple of cattle or a 'hunter' horse for them. The priest took the profits and the farmer bore the costs of rearing those animals.

In some parts of the country, Mayo included, the list of donors was read aloud from the altar, along with the amount donated in Christmas and Easter dues. Some areas went further, with collections being held at the funeral Mass of a parishioner. Again, the list of contributors and the amounts they paid were read aloud for all to hear at the next Sunday Mass.

However, it must also be said that many priests were true leaders of their flocks, attending to their temporal needs, as well as their spiritual ones when the occasion arose. Many deserve honourable mention for their work in Penal times as they ministered to their people, saying Mass, hearing confessions and performing marriage and funeral

ceremonies. There was a reward of £5 offered for information leading to the capture of a priest and £20 for the arrest of a bishop. At one period, the same reward was offered for the head of a priest and that of a wolf. Bribes were offered to all who would betray Catholics.

In the words of an old poem:

> They bribed the flock, they bribed the son,
> To sell the priest and rob the sire;
> Their dogs were taught alike to run
> Upon the scent of wolf and friar.

THE WILD GEESE

England's Penal Laws against Irish Catholics were established at the close of the seventeenth century and grew increasingly more severe as the eighteenth century progressed.

It was said that the Irish clerical students could be easily recognised when they got to the Continent by their red eyes and the smell of turf smoke. Living and studying in damp caves, a good turf fire was needed, regardless of other effects. The fires had to be extinguished during the day so no telltale smoke would give the spies a clue. The students who attempted to reach the Continent to complete their studies were euphemistically known as wild geese; they were leaving the country but, like actual wild geese, they were expected to return.

The owners of the boats that took students to the Continent were usually smugglers, who abounded along the west coast of Ireland in those days. Running the gauntlet of the English navy and the elements, they probably had no more than an even chance of reaching the mainland of Europe in their light luggers, as their small boats were called. The smugglers were the unsung heroes and would help to keep the people's hopes alive in dark and evil days. The ordained priests were taken aback by the fact that the Irish students faced certain death if they were caught in Ireland or, as often happened, on the high seas, in which case, the smuggler and his crew shared the same fate with their ultimate end unknown and unrecorded.

The Oath of Abjuration introduced in 1712 stipulated that all Roman Catholic clergymen who did not swear to abjure all Roman Catholic practices and rituals by a certain date were to be transported and any who returned again would have his life rendered forfeit to the Crown. Out of nearly 2,000 Roman Catholic clergymen of all ranks, only thirty-three, all in poor health, took the oath. The only Mayo clergyman to take the oath was named as Father John Durkin of Killedan parish.

WAKES AND FUNERALS

Many theories have been advanced to explain the old Gaelic custom of playing games at wakes for the dead. All authorities agree that no disrespect for the dead was intended. Very often relatives of a deceased person asked the younger people at the wake to commence the games. Often an old man, feeling his end draw near, gave instructions as to the games to be indulged in at his wake.

The old Gaelic race looked on a natural death as a happy release from the cares and worries of this world to a happier life in the next world. Only when a young person met a sudden or untimely end did they regard death as a cause for lamentation. Until recently, when the last sod of turf was cut, the last sheaf of grain reaped or some other seasonal work completed, God's mercy on the dead was invariably invoked by the people involved in the work.

When enjoying the first sample of some fruit or vegetable such as new potatoes, the usual saying was, '*Go mbeirimid beo ag an am seo arís*' (That we may be alive this time [next year] again).

East Mayo seems to have been one of the last strongholds in Ireland of the custom of playing games at wakes as there are many people still alive who took part in them. The First World War and the troubled times helped to put an end to many old world ideas. Some of those games were just trials of strength or agility, such as 'tug o' war' with a brush handle over a chalked line on the floor or jumping over and back across a stick while holding an end in each hand.

Two of the most popular games were known as '*Thart an Bhróg*' and 'Riding the Blind Donkey.' In the first game, a number of players sat in a circle and secretly passed some small object to each other. A 'victim', seated on a chair in the centre of the circle, was expected to name correctly, who was in possession of the object when asked. The object was often a child's shoe and to mislead the man in the middle the person in possession of the shoe would whisper '*Cuir thart an bhróg*' (pass the shoe). This is how the game got its name.

In the game of Riding the Blind Donkey, two stout kitchen chairs were placed about 4ft (1.2m) apart. A strong spade or shovel handle was placed horizontally with an end resting on the seat of each chair. The operator then had to sit cross-legged on the spade handle. While precariously balanced there, four small objects, such as potatoes or small sods of turf, were placed on the outer corners of the chair seats and he was expected to knock those objects on to the floor with a short stick while maintaining his balance.

The penalties or forfeits for failure in those games varied in different localities. The penalty in '*Thart*' was usually a number of thumps on the back by the strong man of the company. As a concession, the victim might be allowed to hold his open hand palm outwards on his back to cushion the blows. In other places, the punishment might be a number of blows of a knotted straw rope. In Riding the Blind Donkey, the 'punishment' often was to force a handful of *deannach* down the fallen jockey's back between shirt and skin. *Deannach* was a dusty abrasive product of oat milling, and as small oat mills dotted the countryside in those days, there was no shortage of the commodity. It had the property of generating a most unbearable itch on tender skin. Near Claremorris, a small lake bears the name of Loch na nDeannach owing to the *deannach* formerly dumped there.

A game played at wakes around Claremorris long ago was known as '*An Bearradóir*' (the shaver). A number of young men lined up to be 'shaved', each being compelled to take a large mouthful of water and stand with distended cheeks while the barber or shaver gave him a mock shave with a goose or duck quill while intoning the words, '*Bearrfaidh mise mo sheandhuinín go lom, lom, lom*'. This implied that he would shave his client bare, bare, bare. If any client laughed, the rest squirted their mouthfuls of water in his face. Sometimes the unfortunate barber was on the receiving end when his client's mouthful of water exploded in his face.

The playing of those games was not always confined to wakes. Sometimes they were played on the night after a *meitheal*, when people assembled to help a backward neighbour with some seasonal work or when flax scutching or some such work was completed.

When the journeyman tailor came to a village, he usually billeted in some 'ready' house where there were no children to interfere with his work and where he often stayed the whole winter.

At funerals, which usually proceeded from the deceased's home in those days, all the neighbouring young men gathered in some field out of sight of the house of mourning. There for two or three strenuous hours, they indulged in athletic feats: jumping, weight throwing and weightlifting, long and high jumping, wrestling, etc.

There was a keen air of friendly rivalry between opposing townlands and this led to records attained and then broken. Regular athletic or sports meetings were out of bounds in some areas as some landlords did not want land being cut up and trampled unduly by young men whom they described as 'skylarking vagabonds'.

THE MOY CORRIES

The corries of the River Moy, the longest river in County Mayo, were lines of boulders used as stepping stones to cross the river at fords along its course. They had been put there countless centuries ago but were removed in the early 1960s when the Moy was drained and a link with the past was severed forever.

In the townland of Loobnamuck, some miles north-west of Swinford in east Mayo, Mass was celebrated during this period of religious persecution on a large flat rock in a secluded field beside the river. People living on the other side could walk across the corrie stones to attend Mass. When the Moy was in flood and the water levels too high to cross safely, the priest would walk upriver and bless the turbulent water. The worshippers would then fill their containers with this holy water.

Their beliefs may have been simple but their faith was staunch, even up until recent times.

But there were other Christian religions in Ireland since the time of the Reformation and while their combined membership made up a tiny percentage of the population, they wielded power far out of proportion to their number. By the end of the 1700s, it was estimated that 5 per cent of the population owned 95 per cent of the land. This proved to be the high-water mark of the (Protestant) Ascendancy.

The Ascendancy was the political, economic and social domination of Ireland by a minority of great landowners, Protestant clergy and members of the professions. All were Anglicans, members of the

Church of Ireland, known as the Established Church. Catholics and others, such as Presbyterians, along with non-Christians, were excluded from this privileged sector of society.

The 'Report of the Commissioners of Public Instruction', published in 1835, gave details of the membership of different religious denominations in each parish in Ireland. The statistics for the parish of Killedan (Kiltimagh) in east Mayo in 1834 are illuminating.

Out of a total population of 6,162, there were only 17 members of the Established Church and 6,145 were Catholics. No members of any other Church were recorded. This represented an increase of 421 over the 1831 returns when there were 16 Anglicans and 5,725 Catholics. In other words, while the number of Anglicans recorded showed an increase of only one person in the intervening three years, the Catholic population rose by a massive 420. No wonder the report gloomily stated, 'If the population growth continues it is obvious that the economy of this area will be stretched to breaking point to maintain its people.'

THE TITHE WAR

According to the 1831 report, there were twenty-two Anglican churches in County Mayo, serving a membership of over 10,000 people. To add to their sense of grievance at their exclusion from the higher echelons of power and politics, Catholics and other non-Anglican Church members bitterly resented having to pay tithes towards the upkeep and maintenance of the Established Church. The Tithe War was a campaign of passive resistance, with isolated violent confrontations between protesters and the police force between 1830 and 1836. Tithes were payable in cash or kind and payment was compulsory, irrespective of an individual's religious adherence. The annual amount to be paid was assessed as 10 per cent of certain types of agricultural produce.

Eventually, the authorities concluded that the time and expense involved in forcing the payment of the hated tithes was putting an intolerable strain on the resources of the police. One official lamented, 'it cost a shilling to collect tuppence'. The collection of tithes was discontinued but not removed completely until the Church of Ireland was disestablished in 1869.

The amount payable was reduced by a quarter and the remainder was to be collected by landlords in the form of increased rent.

THE CATHOLIC MIDDLE CLASSES

With the relaxation of the Penal Laws, a Catholic middle class started to emerge. While the last of these repressive laws wasn't repealed until 1829, the year Catholic Emancipation was granted, many had fallen into abeyance and Catholics were free to engage in trade and the lower professions and a new class, 'strong' farmers', began to emerge. The term 'strong' did not refer to the farmer's physical strength but to the size of his land holding. Until a number of land reform acts (referred to as the Land Acts) were passed in the late nineteenth/early twentieth centuries, the greater part of the country was owned by a relatively small number of wealthy individuals. Their tenants attempted to survive on tiny holdings, often of just a couple of acres. However, in the aftermath of the Napoleonic Wars, prices for agricultural produce soared and some farmers saw a rise in their incomes. They were able to lease larger, more profitable holdings of land and they came to be known as strong farmers. Their new-found wealth allowed them to build bigger houses than the usual one- or two-roomed thatched cottage.

Furthermore, they began to look for educational services for their children. The Archdiocese of Tuam led the way in Connacht with the opening of St Jarlath's College in Tuam, north Galway in 1800. St Nathy's, Ballaghadereen, in the diocese of Achonry followed suit in 1810. The educational syllabus was narrow and focussed. There was a strong emphasis on the classics, Latin and Greek, and the tenets of Catholic theology.

Such boarding colleges were known as junior seminaries or 'junior sems', because one of the main objectives was to recruit candidates for the priesthood from the student ranks. The vast majority of pupils in a junior sem stayed at the school during term time. One of the reasons for this was that only the relatively wealthy classes could afford to send their children to secondary schools and, since only a small percentage of the population of Mayo fell into that category, the pupils enrolled in such schools often lived many miles from the colleges where they were educated.

Nuns provided girls' education and the curriculum was similar to the standard to be found in junior sems and other types of second-level schools for boys.

The standard of education for the masses improved slowly but steadily throughout the latter half of the nineteenth century and right on up to 1967, when the system of free secondary education was introduced. Still, the conservative nature of Catholic education and religious beliefs remained largely unchanged since the era of the Penal Laws and earlier. The main difference between the customs then and in earlier times was that the faithful could openly practise their beliefs.

Statues of various saints were to be found everywhere, from kitchen mantelpieces to the entrances to every Catholic school in the county – and there were many of those. Shrines, small religious grottoes, were built at crossroads or market places in towns.

Pictures were equally numerous, the iconic one being the Sacred Heart of Jesus in a variety of styles. Few households were without the triptych of US president, John F. Kennedy, flanked by two popes, John XXIII and Paul VI. There was a hierarchy of values when it came to choosing the statue or picture to pray to.

St Anthony was the favourite when someone prayed for the return of lost or stolen goods and St Joseph of Cupertino was the saint to invoke when someone went on a journey. Naturally, there were many for whom Mary, Mother of God, was the only one from whom to seek help. Some prayed to Mary, the Blessed Virgin, while others turned to a representation of Mary, the Mother of God, and there were several other guises under which help from Mary would be sought.

For most deeply religious Catholics, there were differences between the various apparitions of Mary at Knock, Fatima or Lourdes. One could get statues, pictures or medals, not to mention scapulars of Mary of Fatima, Lourdes or Knock. (Up until the power of the Church began to wane in the closing decades of the last century, those three alleged apparitions were the only ones taken seriously.)

Looking back over the history of Mayo ever since the earliest times, one could say that the pisreógs and superstitions that were passed down from generation to generation have finally died out. On the surface at any rate, overt displays of belief in inanimate objects and rituals seem to belong to the past but one can never say that with certainty.

7

BALLINTUBBER ABBEY

> I walked entranced
> Through a land of Morn:
> The sun, with wondrous excess of light,
> Shone down and glanced
> Over seas of corn
> And lustrous gardens aleft and right.
> Even in the clime
> Of resplendent Spain,
> Beams no such sun upon such a land;
> But it was the time,
> 'T was in the reign,
> Of Cahal Mór of the Wine-red Hand.

The poet James Clarence Mangan (1803–1849) was unstinting in his praise of Cahal (or Cathal) O'Connor, the Connacht king who founded Ballintubber Abbey. (*Mór* is a Gaelic term to describe greatness.)

St Patrick is said to have visited Ballintubber in the course of his missionary journey around Ireland, preaching to the people in the areas he passed through. It was his custom to baptise local people using water from a well in the locality. He also founded a small church in the vicinity of the well and this church and the well became places of pilgrimage after the Patrician visit. That is how this area came to be called *Baile an Tobair*, which means the townland of the (blessed) well.

A colourful local legend tells how King Cathal came to have the imposing Ballintubber Abbey built. Cathal was the illegitimate son of Turlough, the King of Connacht. He was known as Cathal Craobh Dearg (Cathal of the Red Hand) as he had a large red birthmark on his right hand. He was said to have been a youth with many excellent qualities and the general expectation was that he would become king when his father passed away.

However, the queen had other ideas. She wished to have one of her sons succeed her husband so she plotted to have her stepson murdered. The boy and his mother were forced to flee for their lives and they came to Ballintubber with the queen's soldiers in hot pursuit. Both would surely have been killed had not the sexton of the church taken pity on them and hidden them until the immediate danger had passed. However, young Cathal's life was still in danger, as Sheridan knew the queen would not be happy until the boy had been found and killed.

So he reared him in secret for some years.

Finally, in 1189, the day came when King Turlough passed away and preparations for the election of his successor began. When Cathal heard the news he removed the glove he had worn for years to hide his birthmark and revealed his identity to all. He was elected king and thus the queen's plotting and scheming were all in vain.

Some time after his election, King Cathal returned to Ballintubber to thank the sexton for saving his life. To show his gratitude, he told his benefactor that he would build a new, larger church to replace the small one that Sheridan looked after.

Here the story takes an interesting twist.

King Cathal then gave his stonemasons precise instructions on how the new church was to be built and left them to do their business. Time passed and one day the stonemasons informed him that they had carried out his orders and the new church was now ready for use. So he paid them for their labours and sometime afterwards, he visited Ballintubber, expecting to see a brand new church in place of the old one.

To his great surprise he found that nothing had changed, the old chapel was still there and there were no signs of the masons' work to be found anywhere in the area. He confronted the masons and angrily demanded to know the reason why they had not carried out his orders. They were as surprised as he was for they assured him that they had gone to Ballintubber and carried out the work they had undertaken to do.

This was a complete mystery to all concerned until someone realised what had actually happened.

There was another sacred well in the province of Connacht, also called Ballintubber. This one was dedicated to St Brigid, who, along with Patrick and Colmcille, is a patron saint of Ireland. It is located in what is now the modern county of Roscommon, about 20 miles (32km) to the east of the Patrician one where Cathal's gift to Sheridan was to have been built. The church builders had gone to the wrong Ballintubber and erected their church there.

On hearing this, Cathal Mór assured Sheridan that he would replace his chapel as promised but this one would be seven times bigger and better than the one built in error at the other Ballintubber!

Incidentally, the church built by mistake in Roscommon lies in ruins today but the abbey in south Mayo is still in continuous use although it was first built almost 800 years ago on the site of another church that had opened its doors almost 800 years before that.

So, if local tradition is to be believed, this is why the very impressive abbey was built on the site of Sheridan's little chapel. It is the only Irish church that was founded by an Irish king and is still in daily use.

CATHAL'S FAREWELL TO THE RYE

There is another story told of how Cathal and his mother escaped to safety when the queen ordered her soldiers to kill the pair of them and of his triumphal return to claim the throne of Connacht when his father died.

As long as they stayed inside the grounds of the church when they came to Sheridan looking for sanctuary, they knew they were safe, as the soldiers would not dare to trespass on sacred ground. However, they also knew that if the queen were to learn where they were hiding, she would have her soldiers mount a twenty-four-hour guard on the church and they would be trapped inside for the foreseeable future.

So Cathal and his mother slipped across the Shannon into Leinster, where they would be unknown, and there he found work as a farm labourer. They remained there for several years. He knew that the queen was still looking for him and that she had spies everywhere so he always wore a glove on his right hand for fear of discovery.

Then as now, people were always hungry for news of what was happening in other districts outside their own. But generally the only way they had of getting news then was by word of mouth. There were news carriers who made their living by travelling about the country, picking up information wherever they could, and relating all that occurred whenever they came to a village or to any group of people who wished to hear the news. They generally received some small payment and perhaps food.

One day, while Cathal and several others were reaping in a field of rye, they saw a man approaching whom they knew as a professional news carrier, or *bolscaire*. So the reapers greeted the newcomer and stopped their work to hear what he had to say. What he told them interested them all but Cathal in particular.

The *bolscaire* said that the King of Connacht had died and that the leading people of the province declared that they would have no one but young Cathal Craobh Dearg to replace him. When he heard this, Cathal stood musing for a few moments. Then, throwing his reaping hook to the ground, he exclaimed, 'Farewell to the sickle: hello to the sword!' He pulled off the mitten and showed his red hand to all present.

'Cathal's farewell to the rye' became a well-known saying in Connacht to indicate that someone had decided on a course of action that was irreversible. He returned immediately with his mother to Connacht, where he was joyfully received, and was proclaimed king in 1190.

Even during the harsh Penal Times, when practice of the Catholic faith was outlawed and a bounty was placed on the heads of bishops and priests, Mass was still celebrated in the abbey even though it was ruined. The faithful would gather in secret at the ruins. Priests lived a very precarious life, as they had to remain in hiding at all times. There were many spies and informers, always willing to collect the reward money or bounty if their information led to the arrest of a priest (£5) or bishop (£20). So believers and clergy alike had to be on the lookout for danger at all times.

Sentries were posted to look out for the approach of strangers or the military while the priest emerged from hiding and celebrated Mass on the old stone altar that had been in the abbey since its foundation.

When Mass was being said, the priest had a boat and a number of able oarsmen nearby. When the abbey was built, Lough Carra was much larger in size than it is today; the waters of the lough came right up to the walls of the abbey. (All ecclesiastical and other major buildings were located beside a supply of fresh water.) In the intervening years, due to wholesale land reclamation and drainage works, Lough Carra has become much smaller.

If the enemies approached, the priest could escape to safety by boat. He could come ashore at one of the secret landing places that were located along the shores of the lake or on the island in the lake where the remains of a 'priest hole' have been discovered.

It is possible that, for a brief period, when the persecution of clergy was at its worst, the habit of having Mass celebrated in secret at the abbey was discontinued. There is no hard evidence that this actually happened but the probability is that there was a brief, temporary cessation. However, that does not gainsay the fact that Mass has been celebrated in this place since the time of St Patrick.

In 1603, after King James I confiscated all religious properties, the Canons Regular, the order that lived in the abbey, was dissolved. The Canons Regular was an order of secular priests, mostly nobles by birth, who lived a religious life according to the teaching of St Augustine.

The roof of the abbey was burnt by Cromwellian soldiers in 1653 and the church remained roofless until 1966, when major restoration work was carried out. Between 1653 and 1966, grass grew up through the cracks in the floor slabs and the building was roofless but the people of Ballintubber continued to worship there.

For more than thirty, years a Passion pageant has been staged in the abbey grounds every year in the week leading up to Easter. Interestingly, all the principal players in the first-ever re-enactment of Christ's Passion continue to play the same roles today.

Truly, a unique church for a unique people.

8

THE GREAT FAMINE IN MAYO (1845–1849)

While poverty existed in every part of Ireland in the years leading up to the Great Famine (1845–1849), County Mayo had a higher percentage of destitute inhabitants than any other county in the country.

A witness at the Royal Commission, over which Lord Devon presided in 1843, stated that 'these people were the worst housed, the worst fed, and the worst clothed of any in Europe. They live in mud cabins littered upon straw; their food consists of dry potatoes of which they are inordinately fond.'

According to the report of the Commission, published in 1845, there were between 1.1 million and 1.2 million agricultural labourers in Ireland whose average earnings ranged between 2s and 2s 6d a week; one half of that number had no work during thirty weeks of the year. Together with their families, they reached a total of almost 2 million people and a half of individuals out of work and in distress.

One of the witnesses before this enquiry said:

The county of Mayo alone could furnish beggars for all England. Many are obliged to stint themselves to one square meal; sometimes a herring or a little milk may afford them a pleasing variety, but sometimes also they are driven to sea-weed and to wild herbs. Dwelling in hovels and feeding upon roots, they are clothed in rags.

Those were the ordinary circumstances of Ireland, and to such a state of affairs famine was now added, with all its attendant horrors, pestilence and death.

In September 1845, a fungal infection struck the potato crop. Much of the harvest was ruined; the leaves withered and the tubers rotted in the ground. It was not possible to eat the blighted potatoes, and for the remainder of 1845, the people affected experienced hardship but few if any people died of starvation.

The following spring, people planted all the potatoes they had. Most farmers were confident that blight would not reappear. However, their hopes were dashed when they discovered that almost the entire crop for that year was affected.

The Prime Minister, Sir Robert Peel, set up a commission of enquiry to try to find out what was causing the potato failures but it was unable to discover what it was.

This was in 1846 and by then, the first reports of starvation began to circulate.

In 1847, the harvest was somewhat better but few potatoes were planted during that spring, as many of the tenants had no seed potatoes left and all were afraid that the blight would strike again. This led to tens of thousands of deaths from starvation and so 1847 became known as 'Black '47'.

There were relapses in 1848 and 1849, causing a second period of famine. In this period, disease was spreading and this ultimately killed more people than starvation. In 1850, the harvest was somewhat better and the worst had passed.

The precise number of people who died during the Great Famine will never be known. The only data that has survived are in the 1841 and 1851 censuses, but their accuracy has been questioned. During that period, it is estimated that over 1 million people died of starvation and disease and roughly the same number emigrated.

PEEL'S RELIEF PROGRAMME

A third of the potato crop was wiped out in 1845. Partial crop failures were relatively common and because of this it was some time before the British Government realised that this failure was more serious than usual.

The solution was to import food but many other European countries also feared famines and had banned exports of food. Prime Minister Peel realised that he would face revolt in his own party if he prevented the export of Irish grain. That would be against the principles of free trade, a key Tory policy.

A law dating from 1838 meant that aid could only be given out in workhouses organised by local boards, called Poor Law Unions. Peel felt that the workhouses would be overwhelmed by the demand so he set up a Relief Commission to organise relief aid.

He came up with his own solution to the food problem. Without informing his own Conservative government, he purchased two shipments of inexpensive Indian corn (maize) directly from America to be distributed to the Irish. But problems arose as soon as the maize arrived in Ireland. It needed to be ground into cornmeal before it could be eaten and there were not enough mills available to do so. This hard, pebble-like corn was nicknamed 'Peel's Brimstone' because of the problems that arose when people attempted to eat it without having it double-ground and boiled thoroughly. In Mayo the term for maize was 'yalla male' (yellow meal) or sometimes 'the yalla buck'.

Yellow meal was difficult to cook, hard to digest and caused diarrhoea. It could be said that the 'yalla buck' certainly lessened the number of deaths by starvation but it could also be said that it brought a myriad of problems that made it a less than satisfactory substitute for the potato.

WORK SCHEMES

Peel also had work schemes set up that were locally funded. At the peak of the famine, over 140,000 people were employed but the rates of pay were very low and workers had sometimes to wait weeks before receiving their wages. The government's key aim was to create employment and around 700,000 people had joined work schemes by March 1847.

The workhouses set up in the previous decade to provide shelter for those in desperate need were strongly disliked by the people. Nevertheless, many had no option but to seek admission to one of them.

CHARITIES

Private charitable organisations kept hundreds of thousands of people alive during the famine years. Catholic priests organised food for local people. The Society of Friends raised money in America and Britain, and gave it to local areas to enable them to buy food boilers. In London, a group of businessmen collected money (including £2,000 from Queen Victoria) and bought and shipped maize to the west of Ireland.

In March 1847, the Public Works schemes were disbanded. Soup kitchens were set up in all but three of Ireland's 130 Poor Law Unions and rations were being given to 780,000 people by May. By the start of June, this number had increased to 2,700,000. At their peak, in mid-August, over 3 million people were being fed by the scheme daily.

The government imported much of this food. Food exports from Ireland reached their lowest level in 1847 and net grain imports reached three-quarters of a million tons in the same year.

However, the government did not spend nearly enough money on the soup kitchens. One distributor of relief at Belmullet, County Mayo, said in May 1847, 'Between today and yesterday, I saw the corpses of a girl, a man and an old woman who died of hunger. This day I saw a woman sinking into a faint, while I was giving out relief at Pullathomas to some peculiarly wretched families.'

But the relief distributor insisted that everything that could be done with very limited resources was being done:

> Placed in the midst of a starving and mendicant population, whom they [the Relief workers] are unable to supply with enough even to support nature, they are liable to continual charges of unfairness, partiality, indifference or want of judgement. It should be remembered that those who thus labour for the poor do so at a great sacrifice of time and trouble, and are in continual danger of being attacked by the pestilence which rages around them.

DISEASE

Diseases, mainly fever and dysentery, arising from starvation and unhygienic living conditions, were an increasingly serious problem.

It was common for doctors and the relief workers themselves to die from disease. Various diseases killed far more people during the famine than starvation alone. Many emigrants brought their diseases with them. An average of 40 per cent of those who emigrated died while en route to their destination or soon after their arrival.

When the potato blight struck again in 1848, most of the harvest of that year was wiped out. But, with the continued improvements to the workhouses, deaths from starvation were not as great as they had been in 1847. Nevertheless, the winter of 1848–1849 was a hard one and disease wiped out tens of thousands more people.

The diseases finally began to wane after the winter of 1848–1849 but the deaths of those people weakened by hunger were still numerous. The potato blight struck yet again in the harvest of 1849, but was not as widespread as in 1848.

WORKHOUSES

The workhouses continued to manage the relief effort, and herein lies the difficulty in determining the exact 'end' of the famine. Many of the destitute found it very difficult to leave the workhouse. The famine ended gradually, with recovery spreading from east to west, as the capacity of the workhouses increased and the number of inmates decreased. By 1849–1850, the workhouses had enough resources to take appropriate care of all the destitute. Emigration also continued, although not quite at the levels of 1847.

The Irish Poor Law Act of 1838 was an Act of Parliament that created the system of poor relief in Ireland, centred on workhouses located throughout the country. The country was divided into districts or 'unions' in which the local taxable inhabitants were to be financially responsible for all the destitute (paupers) in the area. Each Poor Law Union had a workhouse, a place where a family with no other means of support could go to and receive the basics necessary to sustain life.

Conditions of entry into the workhouse were strict and entry was seen as the very last resort for many. Once inside, the inmates were forced to work, food was poor and accommodation was often cold, damp and cramped.

A typical day inside the workhouse was to rise at 6 a.m., breakfast at 6.30 a.m., work until 12 noon, have lunch and then work until 6 p.m. Supper was served at 7 p.m., with final lights out at 8 p.m. A roll call was carried out each morning. Meal breaks were in the communal dining room and held in silence. Husbands, wives and children were separated as soon as they entered the workhouse and could be punished if they attempted to speak to each other. An inmate's only possessions were his/her uniform, mattress and blanket. Toilet facilities consisted of a covered cesspit with a hole on which to sit. Once a week the inmates were bathed and the men shaved.

By the end of 1846, the Great Famine was taking its toll and many of the workhouses were full and refusing to admit new applicants. Widespread shortages of bedding and clothing led to the practice of giving the unwashed clothes of inmates who had died from fever or disease to the next new inmate arriving at the workhouse. There was a shortage of coffins and burial grounds were often located close to the workhouse, sometimes next to the water supply.

Boards of Poor Law Guardians, partly elected by ratepayers, but also including magistrates, exercised the functions of Poor Law Unions. Under the terms of the 1838 Act, Mayo was divided into five administrative areas (Poor Law Unions) which administered relief: Ballina, Ballinrobe, Castlebar, Swinford and Westport.

Four more were opened in Belmullet, Claremorris, Killala and Newport in the period 1848–1852. Although by then the worst of the famine had passed, the scale of devastation was large and widespread; evictions continued and conditions did not improve for many years afterwards. The destitute continued to seek admission to workhouses for years after the potato blight disappeared.

AGRICULTURE

Landlords varied in their reaction to famine events. Some refused to help, taking the opportunity to evict smallholders from their estates. Some did not even live in Ireland. Others landlords bankrupted themselves trying to help their tenants.

The Extension Act (1847) denied aid to anybody owning over a quarter of an acre of land. Another clause, the £4 clause, made the landlord responsible for all landholding tax on any holding valued at under £4. This latter clause covered most tenancies in Mayo. For many landlords the £4 clause provided a motive to clear small leaseholders from their estates. While many evicted these tenants in order to avoid paying these duties, many were nearly bankrupt anyway, due to the effects of the famine.

It was the small farmers, such as tenants-at-will, who nearly all vanished in the years after the famine. Many small landholders had only one-year leases of their farms so their tenure on their holdings was insecure, to say the least, but the tenants-at-will fared even worse. They could be evicted at the whim of the landlord without notice and, effectively, no recourse to law. Many of those who had been evicted emigrated or became paid labourers for other farmers. Large-scale farmers or 'graziers' purchased many other farms.

Many landlords had seen their incomes fall during the famine and, having removed many of their tenants, many more went bankrupt due to lack of rentals. Over the next half-century, most of these estates were sold. Some landlords survived by moving away from potato-growing tenancies and, instead, rented out land to graziers, people who reared and fattened cattle or sheep on grazing land. By the end of the nineteenth century, large parts of Mayo had become grazing areas.

The 'strong farmers' became the ultimate beneficiaries of the famine. With a large majority of the smallholder class gone and a weakened landlord class, they were readily able to acquire lands and extend their holdings.

The government set up the Congested Districts Board to help those living in coastal regions in the west. Initially the board pioneered new farming methods and improved land, but later it bought up and redistributed land. The board had powers to purchase inland estates and divide the land into holdings for people from congested areas. Together, the famine and the Congested Districts Board totally changed the structure of the western landscape. Large parts of Connacht reverted to their original wild state, leaving only the odd ruined cottage and the telltale vertical lines of former lazy-beds.

EMIGRATION

One of the most obvious effects of the famine was emigration. Most of those who left and survived their passage ended up in North America, with some reaching Australia, while a good number settled in Britain.

For transatlantic passengers, there were two ways to travel: either as a standard-class or a steerage-class passenger on a ship. With many of the emigrants suffering from fever, coupled with the cramped and insanitary conditions on board what became known as the 'coffin ships', disease was rampant. It is estimated that perhaps as many as 40 per cent of steerage passengers died either en-route or immediately after arrival. Although they were regulated, many of the ships were privately owned, and some captains grossly overcrowded them in order to get more fares.

Most who survived the trip stayed in the cities of the east coast, where they took some of the most menial jobs. Emigration continued to the USA for almost a century. But increasing numbers went to Canada or Australia as the years passed. Many of the American emigrants brought with them a deep hatred of the government back in Britain, which they blamed for the famine and their suffering.

DEMOGRAPHICS

The emigration that continued for the next century or more had a profound effect on Ireland's demography. The country was transformed by the famine. Only the metropolitan areas of Belfast, Dublin and Cork managed to increase their population. Southern and western areas suffered the greatest falls; Mayo was the hardest hit county in the land, with 100,000 deaths reported for the period 1841–1851 and a similar number of people had emigrated.

There are numerous reminders of the Great Famine to be seen on the Mayo landscape: workhouse sites, famine graves, sites of soup kitchens, deserted homes and villages and traces of 'lazy-beds' on the hillsides.

The Irish language went into decline in the post-famine years. It must be pointed out that the Irish language was already in decline at the start of the famine, but the terrible events speeded up the process. In the early part of the 1800s, around 40 per cent of the population spoke Irish, compared to around 30 per cent in 1845, the eve of the famine. Those who died or emigrated during the famine were disproportionately Irish speakers, mainly because the famine hit rural areas hardest and that is where Irish had survived the longest. In 1861, the number of Irish speakers had fallen to 24 per cent. This decline has continued to the present.

THE RUNDALE SYSTEM

The Rundale System of land holding had been widespread in the west of Ireland since the days of the Brehon Laws and lasted longer in County Mayo than in any other county.

In Mayo it was still in use in some areas until the early years of the twentieth century. Under this system of land tenure, the individuals who farmed the land did not own it. In pre-Norman times, the clan, or extended family, owned the land, whereas in the wake of Cromwell's conquests, the ownership of the land passed over to the adventurers and merchants who had funded his campaign. In time those newcomers grew rich and became known as the Ascendancy, the hated landlord classes. In this system, the landlord in question leased the land to one or two tenants and they were answerable to him. They, in turn, divided the available land amongst all members of the group they belonged to.

There could be twenty or thirty others sharing this common land. It was divided into several sectors, based on land quality. All of the joint tenants on a Rundale holding were assigned at least three parcels of land, reflecting the different quality types. This was the case, in theory anyway, but it led to much internal squabbling and bitterness amongst the members of each holding.

The land was distributed amongst the tenants based on the amount of rent contributed. The different pieces of land within the Rundale holding were shuffled periodically to promote a fair distribution of poor-, fair- and good-quality land. Also, some parts were held in common, such as mountainous regions for sheep grazing or 'infield' areas for rearing suckling calves.

People lived in *clacháns* – groups of cabins in close proximity to each other. The mountainous, boggy areas of County Mayo were ideal places for this type of land use. This poor-quality land was unappealing to the large-scale farmers but, under the Rundale system, where the land was shared by a number of tenants, and the plots for growing potatoes were rotated amongst them, it was possible to insert portions of previously untilled land into the holdings of each farmer.

Besides, the potato is an incredibly versatile vegetable that can thrive on all sorts of soil types, from parkland to peat bog, and so the landlord was able to make use of previously untilled land.

Before the famine, it was fairly common for farmers to subdivide their lands between their sons and often there were several sons to share it. In some areas, this policy was carried to ridiculous extremes, with hundreds of tiny fields often dividing an area of land. After the famine had passed, parents generally left the farm to a single son.

THE GENTLEMAN WHO PAYS THE RENT

Often a pig was kept in a sty in close proximity to the cabin. The manure from pigs and other farm animals was stacked in a heap beside the cabin before being taken to the potato plots. This added to the general squalor

and the unhygienic conditions that prevailed throughout the county. One reason for the proximity of the dung heap to the cabin was to enable the landlord, or his agents, to see if the tenant had a plentiful supply when it was time to spread it on the land.

Pig manure was used to fertilise the land where potatoes were grown. Pigs were fed on small potatoes and boiled potato skins, supplemented by the addition of boiled nettles and anything else that came to hand, such as any oat or barley grain that could be spared.

Many families literally kept the pig in the parlour. The 'parlour' in this case often meant the only room in the wretched hovels in which cottiers and farm labourers and their dependants lived. Other animals such as calves and, indeed, cows could be kept at one end of a room, with the family packed into the remainder.

Pigs were reared for sale rather than food, as the money to be made by selling them was often all a farmer could put aside to pay the rent. With good reason, the pig was known as 'the gentleman who pays the rent'.

9

THE QUEST FOR SAM: THE STORY OF MAYO FOOTBALL

It is widely acknowledged that Mayo is a sports-mad county, especially if the topic under discussion is Gaelic football and, more so, if it is the men's senior football team we are talking about.

Don't worry; we love our ladies also, especially when we are referring to the Ladies GAA team. In a glorious spell, from 1999 to 2003, the ladies showed the men the way to glory by winning four out of five All-Ireland titles, missing out in 2001, when they the were the beaten finalists.

Cora Staunton, probably the most gifted female player of all time, won an incredible total of eight All-Star awards between 2000 and 2013. Helena Lohan, Marcella and Christina Heffernan, Claire Egan and Denise Horan won three or more All-Star awards during that golden spell.

Their male counterparts did not have such luck and still don't. In fact, one has to go back to 1951 to find Mayo's name on the Sam Maguire Cup, the ultimate sporting award in this country. For a proud sports county, the long wait has been unbearable and no one can rationally explain why Mayo has been so unsuccessful for so long.

In 1951, the most successful team to represent the county won their second consecutive title, beating their great rivals, Meath, after a thrilling game. The previous year, they had beaten Laois in a very one-sided game and there was good reason to believe, as they faced into the '52 campaign, that more successes were going to follow on a regular basis.

However, it has been sixty-five years since Mayo last won Sam, as the trophy is known in colloquial terms, and each year the yearning for success gets stronger for footballers and followers alike. But, the list of unlucky breaks and unfortunate accidents keeps getting longer and longer.

Friend and foe alike pay tribute to the determination of the Mayo team and its loyal fans each time the championships get underway and the quest for Sam begins once more. There have been near misses, capricious refereeing decisions and outrageous quirks of misfortune but there have been plenty of years also when the team was nowhere near good enough to get to the final, let alone win it.

For all of that, there is an abiding admiration of Mayo football wherever neutrals are gathered. It is the county most neutral GAA followers would like to see win an All-Ireland title. Mayo has been in seven finals since Sam departed and all have been lost.

Benjamin Franklin once said that there were only two certainties in life: death and taxes. If he were alive today and had even a passing interest in Gaelic football, he would add in Mayo's determination to keep on trying until Sam Maguire re-visits the county.

Mayo won its first All-Ireland title in 1936, after playing in and losing four previous finals. The team finally managed to get over the line, in a manner of speaking, when trouncing Laois in the 1936 final. The final score was 4–11 to 0–5, a margin of 18 points.

A *Western People* journalist was present in Barry's Hotel, close to Croke Park, when the victorious team and the County Board officials gathered after the match. As can be seen, it is written in rather verbose language, in common use at the time:

Scenes after 'All Ireland'
Indescribable scenes were witnessed at Barry's Hotel when a *Western People* reporter visited it after the game on Sunday evening.

War cries were raised as the Mayo footballers, flushed with their greatest triumph, came trooping in and they were subjected to a seemingly endless orgy of handshaking. Bemused and happy, they found their way to their rooms, where they quickly changed.

Scarcely any of the team bore traces of the game, which was little wonder considering that it was the easiest probably of their careers. They behaved like boisterous school children as they made impromptu speeches and executed dances of joy in each others' arms. No less jubilant were the members of the Co. Board, who were smiling broadly. And looked as though life had no more to offer.

Western People, Saturday,
3 October 1936

Apart from the solitary All-Ireland win in 1936, Mayo dominated the National League in the 1930s, winning six consecutive titles, starting in 1933–34.

Mayo players, officials and fans didn't have the same reason to celebrate again until 1950.

MAYO'S GREATEST TEAM

In 1950, Mayo went all the way, beating Louth by 2–5 to 1–6, a margin of 2 points. It was their second All-Ireland win.

The following year, Mayo appeared in the final again; this time the men from Meath, the royal county, were their opponents. The westerners won, scoring 2–8 to Meath's 0–9. Years afterwards, at the turn of the century when the Team of the Millennium was selected, Seán Flanagan and Tom Langan of that Mayo side were selected. Pádraig Carney, another member, was inducted into the GAA Hall of Fame. After the 1951 win, Mayo went twelve years without winning another Connacht Championship title.

The next time Mayo appeared in a final was in 1989. The team, managed by John O'Mahony, defeated Tyrone in the All-Ireland semi-final before getting close to winning an All-Ireland title in Mayo's first All-Ireland final appearance in thirty-eight years, ultimately losing to Cork on a score line of 0–17 (17) to 1–11 (14).

A young, inexperienced Mayo team had put in an impressive display against a vastly more experienced outfit and long-suffering supporters had good grounds for expecting the drought would end, sooner rather than later. After the game was over, a picture appeared in one of the newspapers covering the event. It showed a dejected John O'Mahony with a young Mayo fan at his side. The youth held up a banner, which read, 'John says Keep the Faith!'Somehow or another that message resonated with Mayo people everywhere. 'Keep the Faith' became the rallying call from then on.

It was seven years before Mayo appeared in an All-Ireland final again. This time Meath faced them once more. Mayo supporters began to celebrate after the semi-final was won. The county colours were to be seen everywhere: on houses, motorcars, lamp posts and on a wide variety of farm animals, including dogs, sheep and the occasional donkey.

The team manager and other, wiser minds in the community appealed for some sort of responsible behaviour from the fans as the premature celebrations were interfering with the team's preparations.

Their appeals had only a measure of success and, on 15 September, Mayo faced Meath in the final with the hopes of Mayo people at home and around the world resting on their shoulders. It proved to be a heavy burden to bear. With only twenty minutes to go, Mayo were playing brilliantly and 6 points to the fore – it seemed to be only a matter of minutes until the Sam Maguire trophy would be heading west after a long, painful absence.

The words of an RTÉ radio commentator turned out to be true as he wondered if the Mayo players would be able to handle the pressure as victory came into their sights. Meath began to carry the fight to Mayo. They might be staring defeat in the face but they would go down fighting, as people had come to expect from all Meath sides. Slowly, they began to close the gap and Mayo players, who had been dominant in all sectors, began to panic and lose their composure. The pressure they had been subjected to in the lead-up to the final was proving too much of a burden and they completely imploded.

Point by point, Meath narrowed the gap until, with time almost up, Mayo's lead had been whittled down to a single point. Then unkind fate took a hand in the proceedings. One of the Meath players, Colm Coyle, received possession about 230ft (70m) away from the Mayo goalmouth and, standing almost on the sideline, he lofted a last despairing kick in the general direction of the Mayo goalmouth. As the ball soared upward, a hush descended on the crowd. All eyes were directed on the spinning orb as it began its descent. Everyone realised that what would happen when the ball landed would determine the outcome of this game.

The Meath full forward and the Mayo full back began to jostle for position as the ball dropped lower and lower. The tension was palpable. In their anxiety, both mistook the flight of the ball and it sailed over their heads. The Mayo goalkeeper, John Madden, stood his ground as most goalies would do and the ball finally came to earth about 10m in front of him. The thud as the ball struck the ground could be heard all around the arena. Not another sound was to be heard. Then the ball bounced up and sailed on over the bar. The roars of relief and exultation from the Meath hordes were matched by the groans of despair and disappointment from their western counterparts.

The replay was equally dramatic. Within minutes of the throw-in, a fight broke out in the Meath goal area. A number of players from both sides were involved. The referee, Pat McEneaney, sent a player off from each side and play restarted. Unfortunately from a Mayo point of view, Liam McHale was their player to get his marching orders. He had been the outstanding player on view in the first game and his absence was going to be felt. The Meath man to accompany him was Colm Coyle, the man who broke Mayo hearts in the drawn game, but who, apart from that, had an undistinguished game.

Mayo was to lose the replay under controversial circumstances and McEnaney was the culprit according to disgruntled Mayo players. Some of them, who were interviewed some time after the fuss and controversy had died down, said the referee had entered both dressing rooms before the start to introduce himself and to clarify any issues that might lead to misunderstandings out on the field.

According to a number of Mayo players who met with him, he clearly informed his audience that he would not allow quick frees to be taken.

Coming close to the end of the game, as was the case in the previous one, Mayo were in front with Meath pressing hard. Meath were awarded a close-in free and as Mayo players walked into position, the free was taken quickly and, with the Mayo defenders caught unawares, the ball wound up in the back of the Mayo net. Mayo was beaten once again.

Two members of the 1951 side are still with us and all Mayo followers wish them well and hope they will be with us for many years to come. The determination of players and fans to keep on trying has never wavered, come what may. There is a symbiotic relationship between the players and the fans. Each draws inspiration from the other. Some of the players were in tears when the losing side of 2004 returned home. They never expected or felt they deserved the tumultuous turnout of loyal supporters that welcomed them back to the homeland.

In truth, the same can be said every time the team returned to Mayo empty-handed. As long as each player did his best and went down fighting, the fans were there to welcome them back, disappointed certainly, but proud all the same.

In 2015, Mayo were beaten in the semi-final by Dublin, the eventual champions. It took two games to get a result. In the first game, Mayo appeared to be in control in the closing stages but, as has happened many times in the past, the weight of history overcame them. The burden of expectation proved too much; they lost their concentration and Dublin snatched a draw.

Who knows what will happen in the coming years. One near certainty is that the Mayo team will set out once again with the focus firmly on the third Sunday of September. It goes without saying that the hordes of fans will row in behind them as they have done year upon year.

Strangers to our ways will often wonder what the tight bond of brotherhood is between players and followers and, if a single word has to be used, it is 'emigration'. Mayo exiles are to be found in all parts of the world, driven there by economic necessity or a desire to travel and sometimes both. To keep in contact with loved ones at home and to hide their loneliness and homesickness, many would use their solicitude for 'the boys' as an icebreaker – in the same way others use enquiries about the weather to get over the awkward phase.

Whenever Mayo get to a semi-final, plane loads of ex-pats will wing their way home to meet loved ones and friends and to reminisce about times past as well as cheering on Mayo.

For those who live in the county, the team's progress is a measure of their emotions. It would be nice to shed the second-best tag and to feel that something positive had come to pass, for a change. Emigration and, of late, rural depopulation, have weakened community bonds and decimated rural areas and positive news from any quarter would help knock rough edges off our collective psyche.

It was no wonder then that the more superstitious elements amongst the multitudes of Mayo's followers began to worry that the so-called priest's curse was not just a myth. According to legend, the parish priest of Foxford cursed the Mayo side of 1951, saying that the county would not win another All-Ireland until every member of the winning team had died. He was supposed to have been annoyed when the team members and their exuberant supporters disrupted a funeral ceremony when passing by his church.

Nobody paid much attention to 'the curse' when it first surfaced sometime in the late 1970s but as time went by and the losses mounted, the more superstitious elements began to grow worried. After all, the losses in 1989 and 1996 were followed by five more, up to the present time. Even though another priest, just before the last defeat, announced that he was going to lift that damned curse – that is, if there was a curse to lift. In spite of his assurances, Mayo still lost the game, Dublin winning by a single point.

Someday, the walls of this particular Jericho will come tumbling down and the long, long years of heartbreak and depression will come to an end.

Keep the faith!

10

THE NIGHT THE DEVIL
APPEARED IN TOOREEN

Back in pre-Second World War times, Tooreen, a small village in south-east Mayo, was not a particularly exciting place. (Neither, for that matter, was any other little town or village throughout the county.) The people of Tooreen were, and still are, a law-abiding community who went about their daily routines without any fuss or bother. It is part of the sprawling Catholic parish of Aghamore and, since both are well off the beaten path, little or nothing of note occurred in this peaceful and indeed idyllic part of the county. In the summer of 1939, Hitler was preparing to invade Poland while the farmers of Tooreen were planning to mow their meadows and harvest their turf.

When it became known that a new curate was being sent to the village to look after their spiritual needs, nobody got unduly excited. After all, such changes occurred from time to time; it was just a matter of routine, or so the majority of the people of Tooreen believed, nothing out of the ordinary was anticipated.

How wrong they were!

His parishioners soon found that just about everything imaginable was out of the ordinary in the case of Father James Horan. It quickly became obvious that their new curate was a dynamic personality, to put it mildly. Their new spiritual shepherd concerned himself with issues affecting his flock, emigration, unemployment and the education of young people in the locality. Contemporaries described him as a genuinely kind and humble man. He was popular with young and old alike. It was said that he was also deeply devout and spiritual – a man of prayer with a deep devotion to the Blessed Sacrament.

As the years went by, he worked hard to improve the infrastructure of the parish. The postal service in the area was poor so he arranged a meeting with senior management in Dublin's General Post Office and, thanks to his efforts, the postal service improved. There was no electric power in the area so he got in touch with the department in Dublin responsible for Rural Electrification and very soon there was electric power in the area. Consequently, locals often referred to Fr James as the man who 'lit up' the parish.

Not satisfied with all he had accomplished to date, he decided that something should be done to provide the young people of the parish with some form of activity. Largely because of his hard work and his refusal to let problems of any sort get in his way, a handball alley was constructed. Where others saw difficulties, the good priest only saw opportunities.

The alley was acknowledged to be a success by one and all; here the boys came to play ball and the girls came to socialise with the boys as nature intended and all was well in the little village in the heart of rural Mayo.

But the new curate was still unhappy; something bigger and grander was needed to engender a community spirit in this little village so he spent some time in reflection and an idea was born in his ever-active brain.

At this time, the late 1950s, social life in rural Ireland revolved around dance halls. Every town worthy of the name had at least one such hall. Dance halls were venues where young adults, and, if the truth be told, some not so young ones, came to meet and mingle with members of the opposite sex. The layout of those halls rarely varied; each had a timber floor, a raised platform at one end where the band performed and a small balcony or alcove of some sort where revellers could rest, chat and maybe seek to impress someone they had met on the dance floor. Romeos lined up on one side facing the Juliets who did likewise across on the other side of the dance floor. When the bandleader announced, 'Ladies and gentlemen, take your partners please for the next dance', the gentlemen would charge across the floor in a most ungentlemanly way. Each was hoping to get the lady of his choice to accept his request to dance before somebody else got there first. Then those who had been favoured by the ladies of their choosing would escort their partners out onto the floor and wait for the music to begin. After ten minutes or so, the bandleader would call a halt to proceedings and after an interval of five minutes or so the procedure would be repeated on a never-ending basis until it was time to call the dancing session to a halt.

Father Horan decided that Tooreen needed its own dance hall and, with the characteristic determination and single-mindedness that the community had come to expect, he set about building one. Once again, he led from the front and, as he had a most engaging personality as well as friends in high places, the money was donated, or was raised through a variety of fundraising initiatives and, suffice to say, in a remarkably short period of time, Tooreen had a brand new dance hall.

The humble curate's belief in Divine Providence was evident to all who knew him and in later years when he had been elevated to the rank of monsignor and had been installed as the parish priest of Knock, the whole country came to realise that this man was extraordinary in many senses of the word.

But his deviation from the pathways of ordinary mortals became obvious to all while he was still plain Father Horan, curate of Tooreen. Tooreen's dance hall was a well-run, popular venue for many as the curate kept a close watch over his flock and, as he attended every dance held in the hall, he cast a benevolent eye over proceedings and was quick to intervene if he felt some of the patrons in the hall were getting carried away by the music and the general excitement. In other words, they were not observing the social probities. He made sure that the manners and the morals of everyone present were of an acceptable standard.

However, there were problems to be faced when the hall opened and even the redoubtable priest had to accept that remedial measures needed to be undertaken if the hall was to prosper. Tooreen had its own dance hall but so had every town on all sides of this isolated, rural village.

Getting the hall built and up and running was one matter but getting dancers to come in sufficient numbers to make the venture profitable was quite another. Tooreen faced serious opposition from bigger, better-known halls in the region. James Horan needed more feet on his floor but how he was going to get them there was going to be a major problem. He put his faith in Divine Providence and begged the Lord to come to his aid.

His prayer was answered without a doubt, but it came from a different source and in a form that rocketed James Horan, his dance hall and the whole of south-east Mayo into national prominence.

He had sought help from above but it came from below.

Back in the 1950s, bicycles were the main form of transport and scores of them were to be found outside every dance hall in the land when a dance was being held. Sometimes there would be a tractor or two in the car park as well and occasionally, the ultimate status symbol, a motorcar would be spotted, parked where it would be seen by all. Any Romeo, lucky enough to have a loan of his father's car, knew he stood a far better chance of getting attention from all the Juliets in the hall than any of his fellow men who had only a bicycle or, worse still, the linkbox of a Massey Ferguson tractor, to offer to see a young lady home after the dance.

One individual owned a car and, as he was also good looking, according to some, and knew it; he was never shy when he got the chance to invite some girl he fancied to slip out of the hall with him for a 'coorting' session in his car. There was nothing unusual in this as he had been known to do this many times before but on this fateful night something out of the ordinary happened that put Tooreen on the map and Tooreen dance hall in the black – in the banker's book, that is.

On the night in question, the amorous couple had barely settled down in the front seat when something extraordinary happened. In the words of the young lady, when speaking to a journalist from the local press some days later:

I just lay back to take my breath when all of a sudden I got a mighty puck right between me shoulder blades and it sent me flying, so it did. I turned around and glory be to God, but there he was and him lowering his head to puck me again. It was him alright with his big, black head and an awful pair of horns. I could smell the sulphur so I knew it was him so I took off and ran for me life.

She certainly did so in style, according to eyewitness reports, for she ran babbling and incoherent right across the dance floor and into the arms of a startled Father Horan. Her companion followed close behind, equally distraught. Getting the pair of them to calm down took some time but the audience finally managed to discover that the devil had appeared in the back seat of the car and, furthermore, he had taken grave offence when he saw what the pair was up to.

Father Horan listened intently to what the pair in the car reported and, finally, when a semblance of order had been restored, he asked everyone present to join him in saying a decade of the rosary to pray for divine protection, just in case the malignant entity was still hovering about.

Finally, when the praying had ended and the devil had made no effort to enter the hall, some of the braver elements decided to go and take a look outside, first arming themselves with stout brush handles.

The car doors were open and the back-seat passenger was nowhere to be seen, though a powerful stench pervaded the interior of the vehicle. One of the party said in later days that he decided there and then to amend his ways and never fall foul of God nor man again. It was the realisation that he'd have to endure the smell of sulphur for eternity if he wound up in hell, which made him change his ways.

The news spread far and wide throughout the land and Tooreen became the centre of national attention as press and radio journalists descended on the little village. Sightseers flocked to the place in all manners of transport and the attendances at the dances in Tooreen's hall for years afterwards exceeded all expectations. Whenever Father Horan was interviewed on the subject in later years, he said he could not explain what had happened. 'God moves in a mysterious way, His wonders to perform'; was his stock reply to all such questions, quoting the first line of a hymn by William Cowper.

Many years passed before the devil in the back seat ceased being a chief topic of discussion in Tooreen and the surrounding areas. One and all marvelled at the way Father Horan's plea to the Almighty to come to his aid was answered. The consensus amongst many was that God must have been extra busy at the time so he got his old adversary

to stand in for him. Some had other ideas but they chose, wisely, to keep their opinions to themselves. Tooreen was benefitting from the publicity and Father Horan was very happy indeed as the numbers flocking to the dance hall increased dramatically and remained that way for many years after. He had his prayers answered and that was all that mattered.

Long years have passed since that memorable night and Tooreen Dance hall has long since passed into folk memory; yet despite the passage of time, no one has found the answer to a mystery that has challenged the great minds of our time and times past since that night in June 1958.

Who put the billy goat in the 'coorting' couple's car?

After giving the matter much thought, the bar stool experts from Tooreen to Termonfeckin are in agreement that only one well-known individual could have been responsible for this escapade.

Only one person would have been able to keep the secret from others. Sooner or later, anyone else would have disclosed his or her part in proceedings. No ordinary person would stay quiet ever afterwards; they would have had no motive for doing so. But one person knew that having the devil in attendance at a dance in the local hall would generate huge interest in the hall and the dances held there and he stood to benefit, on behalf of the community, as the admission tickets sold like hot cakes.

Indeed, God moves in a mysterious way, His wonders to perform.

11

SAMUEL LEWIS: THE TOPOGRAPHY OF COUNTY MAYO

The Topographical Dictionary of Ireland by Samuel Lewis (1836) is a valuable source of information on Mayo's historical past. Lewis was an editor and publisher of topographical dictionaries and maps. He produced dictionaries for the United Kingdom of Great Britain and Ireland (Ireland, England, Scotland and Wales).

The purpose of the texts was to give in 'a condensed form, a faithful and impartial description' of each place. For Ireland, Lewis relied on a wide range of sources of information, including, Coote's *Statistical Survey* (1801), Taylor and Skinner's *Maps of the Roads of Ireland* (1777) and, in particular, the census of 1831 and the education returns of the 1820s and early 1830s. Distances are in Irish miles (the statute mile is 0.62 of an Irish mile.)

He frequently refers to civil parishes, local administration units, which are unique to Ireland. They were units of territory that had their origins in old Gaelic territorial divisions. They were adopted by the Anglo-Normans when they arrived in the country. In the nineteenth century, they were gradually replaced by Poor Law Divisions but have not been formally abolished and are sometimes used for legal matters. They no longer correspond to the boundaries of Roman Catholic or Church of Ireland parishes, which are generally larger. To complicate matters even further, the ecclesiastical parishes don't always correspond; in effect, there are three different types of parish in Irish society but the one most commonly referred to at the present time is the Roman Catholic system; for Lewis, the predominant church was the established one, the Church of Ireland.

Baronies are frequently mentioned also. These were ancient administrative units that are no longer used today.

Lewis also mentions tithes (ecclesiastical taxes) and applotments. The Tithe Applotment Books were compiled between 1823 and 1837 in order to determine the amount which occupiers of agricultural holdings over one acre should pay in tithes to the Church of Ireland. Those tithes were levied on non-Anglican landholders no matter what their religious beliefs were.

He collected data from all areas of Mayo and what he published in 1837 gives us an interesting insight into urban life in Mayo in the period leading up to the Great Famine. Some of the entries are short, while others go deeper into the history, geography, anecdotes, superstitions, and the life of the people in an area. References are made to various industries in areas around the country, while civil and religious parishes are identified and churches described.

There was very little variation in the manner in which each entry was prefaced. The one he used when introducing Clare (Claremorris) is reproduced below:

CLARE, or CLAREMORRIS, a market and post-town, in the parish of KILCOLEMAN, barony of CLANMORRIS, county of MAYO, and province of CONNAUGHT, 14 miles (S. E. by S.) from Castlebar, and 117 ½ (W. by N.) from Dublin; containing 1476 inhabitants. It is situated on the road from Ballinrobe to Castlerea, and consists of one long street, containing about 300 houses, principally slated.

Swinford got more or less the same lead-in:

SWINFORD, a market and post-town, in the parish of KILCONDUFF, barony of GALLEN, county of MAYO, and province of CONNAUGHT, 15 miles (S. E. by S.) from Ballina, and 140 (W. N. W.) from Dublin, on the road from Foxford to Ballaghadireen; containing 813 inhabitants. This improving town, which consists of one principal and two smaller streets, comprises 150 houses, nearly all of which are slated.

In some cases, he refers to the gentlemen of the area in question and their residences. In the main, they were landlords or members of a profession. Lewis did refer to the quality of land in some areas and the uses to which it was put but he made no direct reference to the tenants who made up the vast majority of the people in all areas.

This chapter details his descriptions of the six largest (modern) towns in the county, classified by population numbers. Much of the data supplied by Lewis has been redacted here for space reasons.

The number in parentheses after each town's name represents the town's population in the Census 2011 returns. Castlebar, Ballina, Westport and Clare (Claremorris), were covered in greater detail than any of the others, which is unsurprising as these were the top four towns in Mayo, as they are today.

But Ballinrobe was the second largest of the six in 1837, when it had 3,683 inhabitants, compared to the 2011 figure of 8,923. In the case of Ballyhaunis, the sixth and last, a direct comparison cannot be made since the 2011 census records the population of the town only, whereas Lewis gave the combined total of the town and its parish, Annagh.

Claremorris showed a dramatic rise in numbers between 1837 and 2011. It had just 1,476 in the former period, whereas in 2011 the figure is 3,979. Castlebar, Ballina and Westport showed modest increases.

CASTLEBAR (12,318)

Castlebar in 1837 appears to have been a rich and prosperous town. According to Lewis:

> It consists of one principal street nearly a mile in length, from which diverge several smaller streets and lanes; and in 1831 contained 909 houses, some of the best of which are built round the green, which forms a pleasant promenade; the streets are paved and kept in repair at the expense of the county.

Castlebar was a market and post-town. It contained 11,805 inhabitants, of which number, 6,373 were in the town.

It was a garrison town then and this was one of the reasons for the improvement in the town's finances.

The barracks, a fine range of buildings recently erected, and commodiously adapted for artillery and infantry, are arranged for 60 men of the former, and for 24 officers and 565 non-commissioned officers and privates of the latter.

All the military personnel had to be 'provisioned' by local merchants and farmers. As well as that, the soldiers would have spent a lot of time in the various pubs around the town.

Castlebar had been a centre of the linen-weaving industry in Mayo in the late eighteenth and the early nineteenth centuries but the trade was rapidly declining when Lewis wrote about it. Linen manufacturing in Mayo was a cottage industry but when mechanised looms were introduced in Ulster, production in Mayo went into decline:

The linen manufacture, which was formerly much more extensive, is still carried on here; and a considerable quantity of linen and linen yarn is sold in the linen-hall, a neat building at the entrance of the town from Ballina.

There were other commercial enterprises in the town that helped offset the decline in linen manufacture:

> There are a tobacco and snuff and a soap and candle manufactory, a brewery, and a tannery; and the general trade of the town, with the exception only of the linen trade, is gradually improving.

He described the parish also:

> The parish, which is also called Aglish, comprises 13,342 statute acres, as applotted under the tithe act; about 1400 are bog and waste, and the remainder arable and pasture. The lands are principally under tillage; the soil is good, and the system of agriculture much improved.

Compared to the wretched hamlet of the mid-eighteenth century described by Mary McCarthy in *Crime and Punishment*, Castlebar had improved greatly in every sense.

BALLINA (10,361)

Ballina was a seaport, which meant that raw cotton could be imported cheaply and this led to the establishment of a cotton factory in the town.

As Lewis put it, Ballina 'is indebted for the commencement of its commercial importance to the establishment of a cotton-factory here'.

In general terms he was very much impressed by what he saw there:

> The town is beautifully situated on the river Moy, by which it is separated from the county of Sligo, and on the mail coach road from Sligo to Castlebar; it consists of several streets, and contains about 1200 houses, most of which are regular and well built. The river Moy, over which are two stone bridges, is navigable from the sea, about six miles distant, for vessels not drawing more than 11 feet of water, to within a mile and a half of the town. Barracks have been erected, and have lately undergone considerable repair. Races are held at Mount Falcon, generally

in May, on a fine course, the property of J. F. Knox, Esq. Within the last ten years great improvements have taken place in the town; many new houses have been built, and are inhabited by merchants and others engaged in trade and commerce.

Ballina, 'containing 5510 inhabitants', wasn't dependent on cotton manufacturing alone for its prosperity:

A very extensive tobacco and snuff manufactory was established in 1801, by Mr. Malley, who first persevered in opening the navigation of the river Moy, and thus gave a powerful impulse to the commercial prosperity of the town: the manufacture continued to flourish, and in 1809 the duties paid to Government amounted to £8,000.

In rural Mayo during the nineteenth century, the pig was 'the gentleman that paid the rent'. Almost all tenants reared one or more pigs to sell at the nearest market and the money realised went to pay the rent.

Ballina had a local bacon-curing industry, which added greatly to the prosperity of the region:

In 1834, Mr. J. Brennan, a merchant from Belfast, introduced the provision trade, which was previously unknown in this neighbourhood, and erected spacious premises adjoining the river, and commodious stores 350 feet long and 140 feet wide, with complete apparatus adapted to a peculiar method of curing: in this concern 10,000 pigs are annually killed, and after being cured are sent to London; and there are also others which carry on an extensive provision trade. There are two large ale and porter breweries, and two large oatmeal and flour-mills.

WESTPORT (5,543)

Westport was a seaport, had a market and was a post-town also. It had a population of 4,448. Then as now, it was a place that attracted visitors. Lewis was certainly impressed by the layout and general appearance of Westport:

It is of modern date, and consists of three principal streets, and a Mall of large and handsome houses on both sides of the river, the banks of which are planted with trees and afford a pleasing promenade. The total number of houses is 617, most of which are well built and roofed with slate ...

And so they should be; Westport was a designed town.

The current town centre was originally designed by James Wyatt in 1780. The local landlord, John Browne of Westport House, had commissioned him to design a centre where his workers and tenants could live.

There had been another village, Cahernamart, in the vicinity but Browne had it razed in order to make way for his gardens at Westport House.

Today, Westport is the undisputed tourist capital of Mayo but it was a place that attracted visitors in Lewis's time. Very few towns in rural areas had a hotel of any sort at that time but Westport had one, '... a spacious and handsome hotel has been erected and splendidly furnished at the expense of the Marquess of Sligo, who assigns it rent-free to the landlord'.

Perhaps it's understandable why the tourists flocked to Westport:

The approach from Castlebar is singularly beautiful, being enriched with the plantations of the Marquess of Sligo, and commanding a fine view of the mountain of Croaghpatrick, the lofty ranges of Achill and Erris terminating in the stupendous mountain of Nephin, and of Clew bay, studded with innumerable picturesque islands.

Westport did not depend on its tourism alone to keep the economy healthy. The port was a busy one:

The trade of the port, which is of comparatively recent origin, consists in the exportation of agricultural produce, particularly corn, and in the importation of timber from America and the Baltic, and of articles of British manufacture.

Not all the grain was for export. Much was used for brewing and distilling locally:

In the town is an extensive distillery belonging to W. Livingston, Esq., established in 1826, producing annually about 60,000 gallons of whiskey and consuming 9000 bushels of grain; a brewery belonging to the same gentleman, and established by his father in 1800, has very much declined since the reduction of the duty on spirits, but is still considerable; in both these concerns about 150 men are regularly employed.

Some linen weaving was still carried on and, for a change, power looms were employed in the production of cotton as well as linen. However, it was to be a case of too little, too late:

About two miles from the town are the bleach-green and linen and cotton-manufactory of Messrs. Pinkerton and Thompson, in which are 24 power-looms, producing weekly 48 webs of 52 yards each, and affording constant employment to 50, and when in full operation to more than 200 men.

The famine that struck the country in the following decade sounded the death knell for cottage-based spinning and weaving for any purpose and nobody had the money or was willing to invest in mechanical looms.

CLARE (3,979)

Clare, or Claremorris, was also a market town, 'containing 1,476 inhabitants':

It is situated on the road from Ballinrobe to Castlerea, and consists of one long street, containing about 300 houses, principally slated. The market is on Wednesday; and fairs are held on May 24th, June 22nd, Aug. 17th, Sept. 27th, and Nov. 23rd.

He refers to the churches in the town:

The parochial church, a handsome building of ancient English architecture, with a light steeple, was erected by aid of a gift, in 1828, of £831, and a loan of £923 from the Ecclesiastical Commissioners. The R. C. chapel, a spacious slated building is in the town, and there is a place of worship for Wesleyan Methodists.

Ballinrobe got favourable mention as well:

It consists of one principal street, from which two others diverge, and, in 1831, contained 441 houses, of which nearly all are well built and slated, and several are of handsome appearance.

It was also a garrison town:

There are barracks for cavalry and infantry; the former adapted to the accommodation of 8 officers and 106 non-commissioned officers and privates, with stabling for 84 horses; the latter for 6 officers and 96 non-commissioned officers and men, with a hospital for 20 patients.

It seems to have been a busy commercial centre:

A considerable trade is carried on in corn; and large quantities of wheat and potatoes, the latter of excellent quality, are sold in the town. There are a large flour-mill, an extensive brewery and malting establishment, and a tanyard, all in full operation.

He referred to the land surrounding Ballinrobe. It is somewhat surprising that he found fault with the land management system in this part of the county, which is one of the most fertile regions of the county:

The parish, which is situated on the loughs Mask and Carra, comprises 13,504 statute acres, as applotted under the tithe act, of which 7290 are arable, 3888 pasture, 324 woodland, 1120 bog, and 882 acres waste land. The land under cultivation has been greatly impoverished by burning and other defective modes of management, and the pastures might be much improved by draining; the system of agriculture, however, is gradually improving.

On education, he had this to say:

> Two schools in the town are aided by donations from C. N.
> Knox, Esq., and afford instruction to about 200 children; and
> there are seven private pay schools in the parish, in which are
> about 320 children, and a Sunday school.

BALLYHAUNIS (3,008)

As happened in some other instances, the population of its parish,
Annagh, is included with the town of Ballyhaunis. The total number
was 6,885. After the usual introduction giving details of location and
distances from other towns, Lewis describes the well-known monastery:

> A monastery was founded here for friars of the order of St.
> Augustine, and largely endowed by the family of Nangle, who
> afterwards took the name of Costello: it subsisted till the reign
> of James I, and at the commencement of the insurrection in 1641
> was restored by some friars of the same order. The remains of
> the ancient buildings consist only of the walls of a church, with
> two small wings connected with it by arches; on the site of the
> conventual buildings a modern house has been erected, which is
> at present occupied by Augustinian friars.

He found little else of note but did record that there were four annual
fairs, mainly for horses and cattle, held in Ballyhaunis and there was a
weekly market on Tuesdays.

> The parish comprises 16,325 statute acres, as applotted under
> the tithe act: it is principally under tillage; and there is a sufficient
> quantity of bog ... It is a rectory and vicarage, in the diocese
> of Tuam, and forms part of the union of Kiltullagh: the tithes
> amount to £194. 19. 11. The R. C. parish is co-extensive with
> that of the Established Church; there are chapels at Ballyhaunis
> and Tulrahan ... There are eight pay schools in the parish, in
> which are about 390 boys and 230 girls.

Lewis also referred to education, as he did in many other instances. Sometimes, he referred to the numbers of children at school and marked the difference between 'schools' and 'pay schools'.

In 1831, a National School system had been introduced. Its main object was to 'unite in one system children of different creeds'. The National Board was 'to look with peculiar favour' on applicants for aid for schools jointly managed by Roman Catholics and Protestants.

However, none of the religious institutions were happy with this as each wanted control over what was taught in the schools under its patronage so where possible, they built and maintained their own schools, often with subventions from wealthy patrons and small contributions from parents of the children attending such fee-paying schools.

12

AGRICULTURE, COMMERCE AND TOURISM

While agriculture is still the principal source of employment in County Mayo, manufacturing and engineering are the two main industries. They range from precision tool and farm equipment manufacture to pharmaceutical production by multinational companies.

Mayo had a strong industrial base as far back as the early nineteenth century. The Linen Hall in Castlebar was one of several market outlets where drapers could come and purchase linen products. Linenhall Street is a reminder of those times.

Incidentally, the Linenhall Arts Centre, which is located on this street, has a programme of theatre, music, cinema, opera, dance, visual arts and workshops for all in the community. It is Mayo's oldest arts centre.

Agri-commerce or agricultural-based commercial concerns were widespread in former times. Grain milling was carried out in Westport and Ballina and in other centres throughout the county.

There were bacon factories in both Castlebar and Claremorris, both relying on local supplies, to a large extent. Piggeries were to be found in most parts of Mayo but a combination of falling prices and increasing costs led to many of them going out of business in the late 1970s. The Castlebar concern, with its distinctive range of Barcastle products, ceased production in 1985. The Claremorris factory had closed some years before.

Flax growing and spinning was once a thriving industry in Mayo. Spinning wheels were common, both to weave flax into linen and wool

into frieze, which was the most popular type of cloth worn by the working-class people and farm labourers.

Linen production was carried out on a commercial scale with tenants augmenting their income by growing and spinning flax. This had been carried out on a local scale for centuries but a number of factors greatly influenced the expansion of flax-growing throughout the county. One was the influx of Catholic refugees from Ulster in the closing years of the eighteenth century. Those included weavers and other textile workers and they brought new techniques and expertise with them. In the early years of the nineteenth century, flax-growing increased as the demand for sailcloth increased greatly during the Napoleonic Wars. As a result, factory-based spinning and weaving was introduced so that linen could be produced more economically than the cottage-based Mayo industry had been able to do. The Irish term '*túr*' indicates a hill or an area of flat ground where flax, after it was cut, was laid out to dry in the sun. Bleaching is the name of this process. Then the bleached flax was dyed before it was spun.

The woollen industry, which had a longer history in the region than linen, was also run on cottage-based lines. The production of frieze, a rough type of cloth for the domestic market, was the most common product.

In 1891, the Sisters of Charity established the Providence Woollen Mills in Foxford. The mills are still in operation despite many vicissitudes of fortune in the years since its foundation. Its products are well known internationally. Its visitors' centre is one of the most popular tourist attractions in the county.

In a county renowned for its angling facilities, there is also, naturally, a brisk trade in commercial fish products. Clarke Fish Exports Ltd in Ballina is noted for its smoked salmon products; Keem Bay Fish Products Ltd on Achill Island is a producer of farmed organic salmon; Ireland West Seafarer in Killala processes whitefish and there are other, smaller, commercial concerns throughout the maritime regions of the county.

Although agriculture overall is still the principal source of employment in County Mayo, the number of people employed in this sector is declining. According to CSO statistics (supplied by Mayo County Council), there was a dramatic drop in farm numbers between 1975 and 1991. In 1975, the number stood at 24,500 and it had shrunk to 11,000 by 1991.

One consequence of the falling number of active farmers was the amalgamation of two or more units and the upgrading of facilities to increase farm produce; for instance, the days when cattle were walked to on-street fairs are long gone and so are the days of cutting and harvesting of turf by hand. For generations, stretching back to famine times, the pattern of farming in rural Mayo underwent little change. In many parts of Mayo, farm holdings were small, seldom exceeding 30 acres (12 hectares) in size, and, almost without exception, the land was only suited for subsistence farming. Some of the land was easily drained, in marked contrast to the low-lying areas where the soil was peaty, acidic and overgrown with rushes, a grass-like plant that is inedible.

Given the adverse conditions, most farm produce in these regions was for home use only. Most households grew small plots of potatoes and vegetables for domestic use and those who grew grain crops, usually oats, did so to provide food for chickens and straw for animal bedding. Some were in receipt of the 'farmer's dole'. This was a means-tested government subvention to sustain those who could not make a living from their farms. In many cases the breadwinner would go to England for a period each year, returning home when it was time to cut turf and grow crops. Once the main period of farm activity was over, he headed back again to earn some more money. This way of life was the norm from the late 1800s. Conditions did improve gradually, beginning in the 1970s, but the drift of people from the land on a permanent basis was noticeable then and it has accelerated as time passed.

The statistics quoted below are evidence that the social demographics of rural Mayo are rapidly changing and not for the better. The move away from manual labour to mechanised means of production began back in the 1950s with the advent of rural electrification and it has steadily continued since. The statistics in question make this clear. For instance, the number of farms of less than 25 acres (10 hectares) declined from 5,282 in 1991 to 3,188 in 2010 – a decrease of 2,094 during this period.

On the other hand, the number of farms of 100 hectares or more increased from 76 to 154 in the same period. So the trend is towards larger farm units with less manual labour involved. (The number of farms of between 50 and 100 hectares increased dramatically in this period also, rising from 290 to 687.) In this, Mayo's larger farmers are following the same trend as most other farmers in the country: bigger holdings, mechanised methods of production and fewer people employed.

Dairy, sheep and beef farming are carried on across the county but the majority of larger farms are to be found in the central corridor of limestone ground that runs from Killala in the north of the county south as far the Galway border and beyond.

Along the mountainous west coast, the emphasis is on sheep-farming and in this regard, Mayo, Galway and Cork are the major sheep farming counties in Ireland.

Unfortunately, 'rural depopulation', the flight from the land, is speeding up. Facts and figures, such as those quoted above, can be overwhelming at times and serve to cloud the greater picture but it is plain that rural Mayo is being steadily depopulated as the farmers and their families and other land dwellers are moving elsewhere at a much faster rate than ever before.

At the same time, the overall population of the county has been increasing since 1971, as the census returns have shown. The only conclusion is that many of those who move away from the land tend to move into urban areas to look for employment in industry or services.

Agriculture still remains an important industry in Mayo, employing over a quarter of the total workforce and many farmers are members of farming co-operatives like North Connacht Farmers. Such concerns produce dairy products, such as cheese, butter and milk, on a commercial basis and buy in fertiliser and other common products that are needed by farmers. By buying and selling on a large scale, significant price benefits are passed on to its members.

Since the beginning of this century emigration has slowed due to the growth of employment in the manufacturing services and technology systems. This has been part of a government strategy to attract hi-tech jobs to the county. The hi-tech, or high technology, industries are, in the main, multinational concerns attracted by the presence of a highly educated, technically proficient workforce. This in turn relies on the excellence of the educational services in the area, which includes the Galway-Mayo Institute of Technology (GMIT) that has been to the forefront of industrial change as well as the improvement of technical skills throughout the county.

The challenge to improve the infrastructure – road, rail, air and communication services – has been a huge one but there has been great progress in all such areas. The IDA (Industrial Development Association), a semi-state agency, is responsible for fostering industrial growth and enterprise and has been busy since the 1970s with a concerted campaign to attract business from overseas. Part of the strategy has been the provision of advanced factory units in selected towns throughout the county. Those buildings are ready for use, allowing interested parties to move in and begin production at short notice. As a result of the efforts of the IDA, Mayo County Council and other interests, a large number of multinational companies have been attracted to the county.

The outlook for the industrial sector in Mayo is positive whereas agricultural input is decreasing slowly but inevitably, as people gradually drift towards the industrialised zones and production is increasingly confined to large-scale commercial operators, factories in all but name.

TOURISM

Tourism is the major service industry in the county. Mayo is a large county, the third largest in Ireland, and it is also the least heavily populated, so there are plenty of wide open spaces to be found there. As Mayo has the longest coastline of all the Irish counties and faces the Atlantic Ocean for all of its coastline, visitors can expect to see craggy headlands interspersed with sandy beaches along its coast from Killary Harbour at the southern end to the townland of Rathmurphy, on the Mayo/Sligo border.

WESTPORT

Westport was well known for its tourist facilities as far back as the late 1700s. In 1790, the first commercial hotel in Connacht was opened there and it was one of the first towns west of the Shannon to be serviced by the Bianconi Tourist Car Service.

Bianconi was the founder of the first public transportation service. He established regular horse-drawn carriage services on various routes from about 1815 onwards. 'Brian Cooney', as he was known to rural Mayo people, made travel between towns and other places of interest not only possible but affordable also. The standard rate of charge was a penny farthing a mile.

There are four main tourist attractions in Mayo and two of them are in the vicinity of Westport. Croagh Patrick lies about 5 miles (8km) to the south and the other, Westport House, is situated on the outskirts, north-west of the town.

The house, the once stately home of the Browne family, is very popular. According to a report in the *Connaught Telegraph* headed 'Westport House reason 60% of people visit Mayo' (29 September 2015), 'Some £50.7 million will be spent in Mayo and the wider region by consumers visiting Westport House this year'.

CROAGH PATRICK

Further south, Croagh Patrick dominates the skyline. Over 100,000 climbers ascend the mountain each year with perhaps another 150,000 coming to the area to enjoy the scenic views. This most famous Irish mountain has been a place of pilgrimage for thousands of years, long before the advent of Christianity, but it is closely associated with St Patrick. The annual pilgrimage is held in commemoration of the period of forty days that Patrick is said to have spent on the summit in fasting and praying.

Every year on the last Sunday of July, crowds of between 20,000 and 30,000 people climb along its well-worn pilgrimage path to the top to enjoy the spectacular views and maybe to gain spiritual guidance and wisdom for so doing. Many take part in the annual climb on 'Reek Sunday' in their bare feet.

Incidentally, claims are made that Patrick spent his years in captivity on Slemish in County Antrim. However, the Irish antiquarian, Professor John O'Donovan and the internationally renowned archaeologist and historian Liam de Paor, amongst others, have concluded that Patrick's years in slavery were spent in an area known today as Foghill beside Killala Bay.

THE MARIAN SHRINE, KNOCK

According to the website www.chooseireland.com, over 1 million pilgrims visit this world-famous Marian shrine each year. Pope John Paul II visited Knock in 1979, the centenary of the apparition. A crowd of almost 400,000 people attended the ceremonies where he said Mass and delivered a homily.

In 1986, Knock International Airport opened, about 12 miles (20km) from Knock, along the road to Charlestown. There are routes to and from other Marian pilgrimage sites as well as other European destinations.

THE CÉIDE FIELDS

The Céide Fields, an area in north-west Mayo, are where a community of Neolithic farmers once lived. The remains of their settlement was hidden for thousands of years as a blanket bog covered the area over a period of time and the settlers had to move out as their environment changed for the worse.

From the evidence to be found, buried under 6ft (2m) of peat, archaeologists have pieced together a picture of the lifestyle of those who lived here more than 6,000 years ago, before the Great Pyramids of Egypt or Stonehenge were built.

The Interpretive Centre has exhibitions, an audio-visual show and visitors can take a guided tour with experienced guides. It is a very popular site for tourists and, as the Wild Atlantic Way passes through the area, there are often queues of coaches lined up in the car park.

THE WILD ATLANTIC WAY

The establishment of the Wild Atlantic Way, a tourism trail designed to provide visitors with stunning views of the beautiful scenery along the Atlantic coastline, stretching from Donegal to West Cork, has been a major success.

The 1,550-mile (2,500km) route passes through nine counties, stretching from the Inishowen Peninsula in Donegal to Kinsale in Cork. Along the way there are places and attractions, which have been designated as points of interest for travellers. The areas listed in Mayo are the Céide Fields, the Mullet Peninsula, Doolough, Achill Island and Clare Island.

MAYO'S BEACHES

With a long coastline facing the Atlantic Ocean, Mayo has many sandy beaches as well as rugged cliffs.

Blue Flag Awards were awarded to ten of Mayo's beaches at the 2015 presentation ceremony at Ballinskelligs Beach in County Cork. The Minister for the Environment, Community & Local Government, Mr Alan Kelly, presented a total of twelve Blue Flags to Mayo, with a further eight Green Coast awards.

The Blue Flag is a certification by the Foundation for Environmental Education that a beach or marina meets stringent standards of water quality, safety and services, environmental management and environmental education and information.

The Green Coast Award acknowledges beaches which meet EC bathing water quality standards, but which are also prized for their natural, unspoiled environment.

ANGLING

Mayo is famous for its angling. It can be said, without exaggeration, that where fishing is concerned, all types of tastes and needs are catered for.

The River Moy, along with Lough Conn and Lough Cullin, which drain into it, is the best-known salmon fishery in the country. The economies of Ballina and Foxford are heavily dependent on the income generated by salmon anglers coming from all parts of the country, England and the rest of Europe. Good salmon angling, both on rivers

and lakes, is widely available throughout the county, with many famous fly fisheries, such as Burrishoole, Delphi, Errif and Newport to name but a few. The other great lakes in Mayo, Loughs Carra and Mask, also provide good brown-trout fishing. Lough Carra supports an excellent stock of wild brown trout averaging 1.5lbs (700g) and Lough Mask is well known for the large ferox trout taken annually, which often weigh in excess of 10lbs (4.5kg).

The seas around Mayo also support a wide variety of fish species, which provide the sea angler with excellent fishing. Shore fishing is also widely available along the Mayo coast.

Like commerce, tourism is in a very healthy state at present as the face of rural Mayo changes slowly, leaving its peasant past behind and reaching out to embrace its hi-tech, hi-spec future and all that it brings.